BETWEEN HEAVEN & EARTH

WRITINGS OF HIS HOLINESS KAREKIN I

Published by St. Vartan Press

Challenge to Renewal

Essays for a New Era in the Armenian Church

...And the Boat Moves on the Waters

Dispatches from an Ecumenical Journey

❖

*A video documentary of His Holiness' 1996 pontifical visit
to the Diocese of the Armenian Church of America:*

A Father for All

Catholicos Karekin Among His People

❖

Available from the St. Vartan Bookstore
DIOCESE OF THE ARMENIAN CHURCH OF AMERICA
630 Second Avenue, New York, NY 10016

Between Heaven and Earth

A conversation with

HIS HOLINESS KAREKIN I

131st Supreme Patriarch
& Catholicos of All Armenians

By Giovanni Guaïta

ST. VARTAN PRESS
New York
2000

Published to honor the blessed memory of

HIS HOLINESS KAREKIN I
(1932 - 1999)

On the first anniversary of his passing

By order of

His Eminence
Archbishop Khajag Barsamian

Primate

❖

The present volume is an English translation of the original
French edition, published in 1998 by Nouvelle Cité.

The international copyright for the material therein is held
by Giovanni Guaïta; the present edition has been published
with his kind permission.

ISBN 0-934728-39-9

*This book has been made possible
through the generosity of*

Mr. and Mrs. Haig Didizian

❧ TABLE OF CONTENTS ❧

Foreword

GRAZ, AUSTRIA, JUNE 24, 1997: Day Two of the Second European Ecumenical Assembly. His Holiness Karekin I, the Catholicos of All Armenians, is scheduled to give the inaugural address. Dressed in the traditional Armenian black robes and monastic hood, His Holiness starts his speech confidently, in perfect English:

> I live in Armenia, the land of Mount Ararat, where for more than seventeen hundred years the people have loyally borne witness to Christ...

In his speech, the head of the Armenian Church analyzes the monumental changes that have taken place in Europe during the past decade. He speaks about the impact these changes have made on the Church. The conference attendees are impressed and captivated by the sharpness and depth of his analysis, his sincerity in presenting the problems, as well as the openness and optimism of his suggestions. Later that day, his answers to journalists' questions during a press conference were even more engaging.

I was personally captivated by his positive presentation on ecumenism, and the fact that such a call for dynamism, such a challenge to modernity, should come from a representative of an Eastern church—indeed, from one of the oldest churches in the world.

I have lived in Moscow for more than ten years. For twenty years the Russian church and Orthodoxy in general have been central to my interests, thoughts, and research. I know the difficulties that the Orthodox churches in the former Soviet Union have had to overcome in face of vast social and economic changes. For that reason, the spirit of openness and optimism displayed by Karekin I inspired me to pursue this interview.

❖   ❖   ❖

Karekin I, the one hundred thirty-first Catholicos of All Armenians, was undoubtedly one of Eastern Christianity's most vibrant twentieth-century personalities. This son of the Armenian diaspora, born to a simple Christian family in a remote Syrian village, studied at Oxford, became Catholicos of the See of Cilicia in 1977, and Catholicos of All Armenians in 1995. During his all-too-brief tenure at Holy Etchmiadzin, His Holiness was able to accomplish many things. He reformed the system of educating future clergy, created centers of religious education for the people, multiplied the number of religious parishes in Armenia and the former Soviet Union countries, opened seminaries, consecrated newly renovated monasteries, organized social service agencies for the poor, sick and needy, and encouraged the Church to participate in the cultural life of the country. He preached extensively, utilizing the mass media; he traveled to parishes, sought out ordinary people, received visitors from different parts of the world. He communicated with politicians, businessmen, artists and intellectuals. His extraordinary energy and work ethic surprised many. But above all, he insisted that "the Catholicos is a servant, who has to go and be among the people, as Christ did. The Church cannot be a stagnant institution. Today it must be dynamic."

Since his early years of service he was involved in the dialogue among the churches; he made it his goal to search for unity among all Christians. His joint statement with Pope John Paul II on Christology brought a ray of clarity to a centuries-old argument. Undoubtedly, this and many of his other initiatives will remain lasting achievements in the history of the Armenian Church. At times he found himself in disagreement with those around him, but he was always open to dialogue, always articulate in explaining his positions, always forthright in accepting responsibility for the greater welfare of the Church. "History teaches us," he would say, "that many decisions misunderstood in their own day, went on to obtain significant meaning with the passage of time."

A prolific writer, his extensive research led to the publication of *The Council of Chalcedon and the Armenian Church,* and he was without doubt one of the most prominent Eastern theologians. Nevertheless, he considered himself to be, first and foremost, a pastor. That is why throughout this book he answers all the questions in clear and simple language. During our conversations, besides the Armenian Church, we touched upon various aspects of Christian faith, including life in the contemporary world, morality, ecology and technological progress.

He always gave sincere answers to my impromptu questions, and in transcribing our dialogue I wanted to preserve the spontaneous and relaxed style of our conversation. The Catholicos never declined any of my questions; he answered them all without hesitation. The extemporaneous nature of the interview did not hinder him from speaking beautifully, even poetically—for example, when he spoke of suffering. As for me, in asking provocative and bold questions, I strived to convey the perspective of an ordinary person who is not trained in theology. My conversational partner accepted all challenges.

Today Catholicos Karekin is no longer with us. He passed away on June 29, 1999. Re-reading some of my questions to the Catholicos, I cannot help but experience an unexplainable feeling—almost a feeling of fear. Of course, had there been any sign of the terrible disease which in a very short time, after indescribable pain, took his life, I would never have asked him what he would say to a person with an incurable illness. Nor would I have asked him to formulate his "spiritual will." But during the exhilarating week when we concluded the recording of our conversation, neither one of us suspected that a new chapter was opening in his life.

When I referred above to a feeling of fear, what I meant was the *fear of the God*: the feeling you get when something unexpected happens, and you realize that Someone has been governing your life. Looking back, remembering my conversations with the Catholicos, I cannot help but think about the mysterious and inexplicable ways of the Lord. Had I not suggested conducting an interview with His Holiness at the time I did, this book, originally published in French, would not exist. Today, I feel sorrow for having lost a person who, without a doubt, was a true witness to the faith of Christ. But I am consoled to know that through this volume, the Catholicos did indeed leave us a "spiritual will."

By God's mercy, the French edition was published in Catholicos Karekin's lifetime. He read it many times and was pleased that it was being translated into Armenian, Russian and English. Having served in the 1970s as an archbishop in New York, he was particularly happy that an English edition would be published. Well-acquainted with life in the United States, he would say that he "felt completely comfortable in America." He identified with the community in America—for which (in my opinion) he had a special affection. We finished the book in New York, where the Catholicos was undergoing medical treatments, and he wrote to me several times afterwards about the importance of an English translation. In this way, the present edition, although published after his death, is the fulfillment of one of his last wishes.

In these pages, the leader of the Armenian Church openly and broadly discusses many issues concerning the Armenian Church and nation. The Catholicos was aware that this was in many ways a novel opportunity for someone in his position, and as a result this book became a platform for him to address Armenians scattered through-out the world, especially those who no longer know the language of their ancestors.

Very few studies about the Armenian Church exist in Western languages. Often the layman's vision of Armenia does not go beyond Noah's Ark and the recent sufferings of this nation. Thus, if on the one hand this book strives to fill a cultural vacuum, on the other hand it may be of interest to historians, Armenologists, and theologians.

❖   ❖   ❖

For Karekin I, human life was *"an encounter between heaven and earth."* These were the dimensions of his theology and spirituality, their focal point being Christ: "God engaged in human history." My conversational partner brought this orientation to every problem we discussed. At the same time, he always expressed a profoundly Christian point of view, never falling into vague spiritualism or clericalism. Hence, the reader — even a non-believer — can, through the prism of Armenian history and the personal experience of the late Catholicos, find genuine inspiration in the words of Karekin I.

Finally, I hope this book becomes for the reader what it became for me: an opening to the spiritual wealth of one of the most ancient churches in the world, and a chance to meet and open-heartedly communicate with His Holiness Karekin I: the pastor, the Christian, the elder brother.

Giovanni Guaïta
Moscow, June 2000

Human life is an encounter between heaven & earth...

—His Holiness Karekin I

First Encounter

In the steps of the Master

Your Holiness, you are the Catholicos, the Supreme Patriarch of all Armenians. According to our theology (common to the Orthodox and to Catholics) you are a successor of the apostles. Two thousand years ago, Jesus of Nazareth, while walking along the bank of the Sea of Galilee, saw some fishermen, looked at them in the eyes, and said, "Follow me." And these men committed a courageous act: they followed this leader, this leader who they did not yet know was the Son of God.

Two thousand years later, you repeat the same experience of the apostles. What does it mean to follow Jesus for a bishop, a successor of the apostles?

To follow Jesus means to walk in the wake of the life of prayer, of communion with the Father, of service and of the teachings that Jesus, the Lord, has passed on to us by His example. There are three elements in the act of following Christ. First, one must feel that one is responding to a call. To be a bishop, a successor of the apostles, is not a personal choice; it is the answer to a call. He who inherits

Absolutely. Often, when one has important and difficult decisions to make, one feels alone. You know that what you decide will have consequences, positive or negative, in the lives of your people... But you must be courageous, and ask, with humility, for the help of God. If I make a decision that has negative consequences, I suffer a great deal. But that is a part of our vocation, to accept success and failure. I always hope that my failures are not too harmful to the Church, and I ask God to fix all of my mistakes.

When I was still a young priest, I learned an important principle from one of our bishops. He said, "Human wisdom consists in making the distinction between what is important and what is less important, or not important at all." One must know how to distinguish the general from the particular. When one makes decisions for the Church, it must be in the general interest. This principle has influenced many of my decisions. One must have the ability to discern a hierarchy of values; he who makes a decision must be able to see everything and to choose what is important. This may not be understood in the present; but history has taught us that certain decisions that were not understood at the moment they were made have been revealed to be of great importance. That is why it is necessary to be courageous: to make decisions according to one's conscience and to assume the responsibility of their consequences.

The Word becomes Life

What does the Word of God mean to you?

For me, the Word of God is a person, Truth incarnate, the Logos. In that respect, one must always make the distinction between the singular and the plural: between the Word of God, who is Jesus Christ, God Himself made man, and the *words* of God, those that we read in the Sacred Writings, placed there in writing by men.

In our world, there is an abundance of words; perhaps too many. The myriad words that we speak every day, and which pass immediately; written words, which last longer, since, as the adage goes, speech flies, but writing stays. But there is yet another category of words, those that become life, words incarnate: those are the Christ-like words. I think that the Christians of the world should understand that the Bible is not an exhibition of a conceptual, theoretical truth, a philosophy, but the manifestation of the will of God that must be translated into concrete acts.

The Word of God is something extremely concrete which must affect our lives. The Bible is not a book of notions; it's a source of inspiration. One would not know how to read the Gospel as an ordinary book; one must look at it as a mirror in which our reflection must resemble the image of Christ. It is in this way that the reading of the Word of God can engage a person, give passion to life, hope to the desperate, and courage to those who are resigned.

Thus it is necessary to live the Gospel. God himself said that His words were "spirit and life," and compared those who listened to His words and put them into practice to a man who built his house on a rock. However, in the Gospel, there are command-ments, Jesus' requests, which are difficult to live by. Certain exegetes see in these expressions a symbolic hyperbole due to the literary genre. Do you believe that one can truly love one's enemies? Turn the other cheek? Hate one's own life?

First, I would like to say that one must make a fair inter-pretation of the words of Jesus. When He tells us not to hate our enemies, in my opinion, it is not a question of feelings or tastes; it is a call to not act like the enemy, to not oppose ourselves with hatred to someone that we hate, but to overcome his attitude of hatred. This love has nothing to do with demonstrating affection or a predilection that one does not have. It concerns an appeal to magnanimity. Thus it is very important to correctly interpret the words of Jesus, to understand them in their context.

Nevertheless, there are certainly difficulties in what Jesus asks of us. But who says that life is a walk in the park? Jesus himself never promised an easy life to those who followed Him; on the contrary, He spoke of the cross and of the yoke, and His cross is there to demonstrate that everything is not so easy... In the Old Testament also, the chosen people had to suffer many tests.

What I mean is that it is naive to think of life as a peaceful river that flows slowly; that would be boring! There are difficulties, obstacles, and problems; because we are human beings, we can fail, fall, and commit sins. But the goal is to transcend this state of imperfection and the fall, since at every moment we have the opportunity to change ourselves. God asks us to do things that are, without doubt, difficult, but not impossible, since He knows our human condition very well. If you commit a sin, you do not stop being the son or daughter of God. Similarly, we must also hate the sin, but love the sinner...

God and thy neighbor

One day, someone asked Jesus what His first commandment was. As you know, Jesus answered, "You will love the Lord, your God, with all your heart, all your soul and all your mind. This is the first commandment. The second is similar: You will love your neighbor as you love yourself" (Mt 22:37-40). What does it mean to love God and your neighbor?

These two commandments are, in fact, inextricably linked. One cannot love God if one does not love one's neighbor; this is, as you know, what Saint John teaches us in the sublime passage from his epistle (1 Jn 4:7-21), in which he says, among other things, "If we love each other, God is in us, and his love, in us, is accomplished" (1 Jn 4:12). God manifests Himself in the men and women He has created, and love for God is never exclusively vertical, but also horizontal. These two dimensions of love complete each other mutually; they are in a relationship with each other like the sun and its rays. As there is no sun without its rays, there is no love for God without love for your neighbor. That is why I do not stop stressing that the love of God passes through the love of men.

But if loving God means loving one's neighbor, doesn't that mean that religion, in essence, is no more that an ethic? One could say that faith, the love for God, is nothing but philanthropy, a dedication to humanity and nothing more.

What I said is that God is not separated from his creatures. If one separates God from men, you get ethics on the one hand and philosophy on the other. But the Christian faith is a concrete faith, and not abstract. Surely, there is also a mystical side to religion, that feeling of the presence of God within us; but one cannot keep that feeling solely for its own pleasure, for that presence leads to others: the incarnation of the Son of God is the ultimate illustration of that truth. It is true that Christianity is also a doctrine, faith in the Supreme Being; but, this Being who is both Creator and Father, our faith in Him cannot be solely intellectual, but it must manifest itself in everyday life, and be realized as an ethic. Thus, for Christianity, dogmatism cannot be separated from ethics. The conception of God engenders a certain conception of man and of the relationship between men. That is where you find the difference between religion and philosophy.

Many of our contemporaries see a moral doctrine in Jesus of Nazareth's teachings, surely among the most elevated and demanding, but not necessarily a religion. There are those who accept the teachings and ethical example of Jesus, without believing that He is the Son of God. Those people seek to conform to the ethical norms of the Gospel without being believers.

I think that that attitude is a little unrealistic. Someone who believes in ethical precepts must naturally ask himself where they come from, if they are the result of an intellectual effort, a sort of pact accepted by the members of society, or if they are derived from an absolute authority. If that absolute authority does not exist, ethics become a matter of relativism. With such an approach, certain precepts of the Gospel could easily be contested, as they are today.

Thus, beyond what the people of our times accept or do not accept, the issue is that you cannot give an absolute value to the totality of the principles of the Gospel without recognizing God in the person of Jesus, the Supreme Being, the entire Truth from which these ethical precepts emanate. If religion is no more than a way of life, then there are no more absolute rules, no distinction between good and evil. This moral relativism is, in my opinion, one of the greatest dangers of this era.

I believe that man must rediscover that feeling of submission to Someone who is incontestable; we are not the supreme masters of the cosmos, we are the beneficiaries and not the source of every benefit.

Thus, if I understand correctly, for you it is impossible to love God without loving men, but really, it is also impossible to love men if you do not have a relationship with God...

I would rather cast that equation in positive terms: if you love God, you cannot *not* love man, whom He created; and if you love man, you love God, because, even if you do not recognize it, in man, you find God.

Then that means that those who have difficulty finding faith but who, in good faith, love men to the best of their ability, will, sooner or later, meet God.

I think so. What I would joyfully add is that there is, among the youth, an aspiration to the life of prayer, of meditation; and if some of them, as you noted before, follow yoga or non-Christian philosophies, many others turn toward charismatic movements, which through liturgical life and prayer, go back to the true source of morality. In fact, in many movements today, people are finding the source of a sound, moral life. And so it is necessary that we, the churches, open up liturgical life to the people.

Unfortunately, in our Church today, the people have become no more than spectators at liturgical functions. Sometimes, it is as if there was an intellectual and spiritual wall between the altar and the nave of the church. We must demolish that wall; the followers must not only listen to our prayers, but must speak them, and participate in the liturgy. For the last few centuries, we have relegated the duty of singing prayers to the choir; but it was not so in the beginning. Today we must make an effort to teach our followers to pray, and to pray together, in communion. What is a liturgy without the participation of all of the people in attendance? Often, when I attend a liturgical ceremony, I invite followers to recite the Creed, the *Our Father*, and other prayers together; everything is different, the church is filled with an atmosphere of community. The liturgy is not a show, but an act that is realized in the spirit and the context of community; one cannot be passive there.

Eucharist, confession, sin

You are talking about prayer in church. For the Orthodox, Catholics and many Protestants, the most exemplary form of liturgical prayer is the Eucharist. What does the Eucharist mean to you?

The Eucharist is the participation in the life of Jesus, and I would like to use a stronger word: it is the reincarnation of God in the life of men. In the liturgical, eucharistic act, you are not living the presence of God as if it were the commemoration of a historical figure; it is as if He descended once again into the church to join us, as He joined His disciples during His life on Earth.

I remember my grandmother. She was a very simple woman, without education, illiterate; but when she took me to church with her, I had the impression that she was no longer the same person, as if she had been transfigured. The Eucharist, which is the very heart of our liturgical life, transfigures us, makes us feel that Christ has returned to our lives, that He is there, as He was with the apostles at the last supper in Jerusalem.

Each time that I personally celebrate the liturgy, I feel that it is not me at the altar; it is as if I am being led by a presence within me, the presence of Christ; I feel that I am no more than the link between God and the people. In our Armenian liturgy, there is a prayer sung by the choir right before the kiss of peace that precedes the consecration:

Christ appeared among us;
God, who is the essence of being, has taken hold here.
A voice announcing peace has rung,

the order of the sacred kiss has been given.
The Church has become a single person,
the kiss has been given as a link to perfection.
Enmity has retreated,
love has spread within us.

All of the Eucharist is there.

*Confession, at least in the West, is a sacrament in crisis; many
people, including practicers, think that it has more to do with
psychotherapy than with religious life; consequently, they say,
it's better to follow the advice of a psychoanalyst, who is competent in these matters, than the advice of a priest who cannot be
competent. How do you understand confession?*

In my personal experience, developed within the tradition
of the Armenian Church, confession is an act of opening
oneself up to God. Our pastoral tradition does not take the
form of private confession as it is practiced in the Roman
Catholic Church. For us, confession is a communal act: the
priest, the deacon or the layperson reads a list of sins and
the followers, who stand around the person, repeat: "We
have sinned against God, forgive us." At the end, the
priest reads the prayer of absolution. If a follower wishes
to have an individual confession, private, it is not forbidden; but in the practice of the Church, it would be an
exception. In monasteries, they used to practice individual
confession, and we have canons that give instructions to
the confessors or followers who confess.

But confession is above all a person's act of contrition;
it is the awareness that one has made a mistake and then

the feeling of spiritual relief. For us, confession normally takes place during the liturgy and is always followed by communion. Thus, when one presents oneself at the altar to receive communion, that moment is the apogee, the sublime moment of that act of purification. The person who opens himself up to God feels that God has heard him, and that through the priest he is forgiven. That feeling of spiritual gratification is the true meaning of confession.

I think that there is a radical, qualitative difference between psychotherapy and confession. Naturally, psychotherapy can help people, but it cannot give that feeling of spiritual gratification, that feeling of being touched by God.

What is in your opinion the gravest sin? In the past, they used to say that sins affecting emotional and sexual life were the most serious...

I have a different perspective. I think that the gravest sin is indifference, apathy, insensitivity. Because that is the very negation of being human.

In our Church, we have a list of sins, in which there are mortal sins, venial sins... But the Gospel says that a sin committed against the Holy Spirit is unforgivable; and that is when, because you have shut out the world, you do not accept the Spirit, you cannot hear the Holy Spirit. That is exactly how I define the word indifference. In my sermons I often repeat: the Church enumerates the seven major sins, but there is an eighth sin, the sin of indifference! Man shuts himself off, he does not want to open himself up to God, and, in doing so, cannot be open to others, he cannot be involved. God is a God of involvement: the incarnation is the involvement of God in human life. Thus the man who is not involved with others rejects the very foundation of the Christian faith, which is a sort of commitment of love. The enumeration of sins in the texts of catechetic and liturgical literature is intended to help the followers of our Church to recognize their faults. But we must never forget that the common denominator of all sins is the estrangement from God, man's alienation from his own nature and vocation, imbued with the image of God.

So you think that indifference towards God engenders an indifference among men.

Yes. It could also happen the other way: it might begin with an indifference toward others; but being indifferent toward others, to be closed off, concentrated on oneself, is a sin against God. God did not create us for ourselves, but for all of humanity. And that communion, that sense of community is the Church itself. That is why I consider indifference a very serious sin; and in our times, people are often indifferent. "Passing by" others, feeling no concern for your neighbor is to deny oneself as a human being.

Thus, sin has a social dimension. One cannot separate the individual from the social realm. Let us not forget Aristotle's lesson: "Man is a social animal."

The Mother of God and the saints

An important part of the life of prayer of a Christian from the Orient is devoted to Mary, the Theotokos, the Mother of God.

Pope John Paul II's motto is Totus tuus, *"I am completely yours," which is addressed to the Virgin. Who is Mary of Nazareth to you?*

She is the embodiment of the Mother of God. Let us not forget that she is a human being; but chosen by God for her purity, she became the Mother of God. It is the greatest glory that a human being could have: to be the Mother of Him who is eternal, He who is the Logos. One of our most popular liturgical chants addresses the *Theotokos* with marvelous words:

> Holy Mother of the admirable Light
> Who holds in her breast the God of all eternity
> And who engenders the Word of God, joy of the world
> We implore you to intercede for us.

In our Church we have many occasions dedicated to the Virgin and there is a profound devotion to her. The Assumption, for example, is one of the five most important occasions in the liturgical year.

The Assumption, which you might call Dormition, as do the other Christians of the East...

No, the Armenian expression *Verapokhoum* means exactly the assumption into heaven. But in our Church, as in other Orthodox churches, we have not made it a dogma. The Virgin is profoundly present in our spirituality, in our life of prayer, but we do not have the dogmatic formulations surrounding her. We emphasize her maternity before all else. Maybe in the West, that is less strongly noted than in our tradition. It is not only the act of giving birth to Christ that is Mary's glory; she raised him and suffered deeply for His absence during His years in public life, when Jesus was so involved in preaching. But in the end, when she knows of the offense done to Him, when she sees Him crucified, she is always with Him. I have often thought about the fact that Jesus' last thought at the final extreme moment of His life on Earth was addressed to His Mother, when he commended her to Saint John. Maternity does not only mean giving birth to someone, but showing love. A mother takes care of her son, a mother gives herself entirely to her son. In that perspective, for us, the very notion of family is centered on the mother. It is, I think, the influence of the Sacred Virgin. An Armenian Catholicos used to say: "A family is like a church whose priest is the mother."

We will return to that issue when we talk about women in the Church. Now I would like to ask what sainthood is to you. Who are the saints?

The saints, to me, are the interpretation of the Christian faith in the context of lived, human life. People often interpret biblical texts through studies or commentaries. The saints are the men and women who interpret the Christian faith in their concrete, everyday lives. In these people, there is a reflection of the Holy Spirit.

In classical hagiographic literature, the dominant feature is that of the miracle, which bears witness to the supernatural side of the lives of the saints; but this is to the detriment of the human aspect, which is diminished. I think that today, we must present the lives of the saints in a new way. The saints are not people who have never committed sins—they are not strangers to ordinary life and have known failure. For example, think of Saint Augustine, of the mistakes he recounts in his *Confessions*. A saint is not an exceptional person, in the sense that he is not like us, since that would mean that we could not be like him. There are many saints all around us, who share our everyday lives, who are not yet recognized as saints, and who may never be, because they remain unknown; but canonization does not make the saint. Personally, I am convinced that Mother Theresa of Calcutta is a saint; and even is she was not canonized, she has inspired sainthood among men, through service, and action. This tells us that sainthood is not detached from real life: on the contrary, it requires a total engagement. Daniel-Rops has a very nice expression, which says, more or less, "I cannot respect pure and saintly hands that have always been protected by gloves. I prefer hands that have remained pure in mud." That is why sainthood is not disengaged, not separated from the life of men. On that matter, there is a very nice expression by the former secretary-general of the United Nations, Dag Hammarskjöld, the great international political personality. In his notebook, published in English under the title *Markings* after his tragic death in a plane crash, he wrote: "In our times, the path to sainthood passes necessarily through the world of action."

We have discussed many aspects of the Christian faith. I would like to ask whether your faith has known doubt, confusion, hesitation. And, if that is the case, how have you overcome those crises?

Yes, I have experienced such moments. Doubt is a part of human life. There are times when you are overcome with doubt, when you are tempted by a feeling of uncertainty, confusion, even by a sort of spiritual depression, the awareness that you have not accomplished all that you should have, despite all of your efforts. Thank God, these crises have not been moments of despair for me. What has helped me is the belief that even if we are impotent, God is all-powerful. It is necessary to see those moments as tests. When you have overcome those difficulties, if you are looking at it correctly, you realize that you have become even more dedicated. I have known moments of doubt so strong that they have prevented me from going about my daily life; I was overwhelmed with doubt. In that case, there is only prayer, the Bible, and, especially, the words of Jesus, which are still a source of inspiration; sometimes all it takes is one sentence or a small passage from the Gospel.... It is the principal way in which we can comfort ourselves and get back our strength. Another way is the one I have found in the lives of saints or of people who have overcome similar experiences of temptation or abandonment.

What is happiness?

Your Holiness, are you a happy man?

I cannot answer that question without making sure that we understand the word "happiness" in the same way. If you are talking about a continuous state of mind, a permanent interior disposition where there is no regret, no suffering, no feeling of dissatisfaction, that state is foreign to me. But I believe that that state of mind is simply not human. In human life, happiness is a victory: the overcoming of doubt, despair, temptation. If this is how you understand happiness, then yes, I am happy because I think that with the help of God, I have been able to conquer those moments of treason. Those who have not lost a sense of the presence of God within them and in their lives are happy. If one rereads the Beatitudes that Jesus established in the Sermon on the Mount, one sees the poor, those who suffer, those who are persecuted are "happy." Why? Because the spirit of God is in these people, despite the negativity they experience; and it is this feeling of the closeness of God and of one's belonging to God that creates happiness.

There, you are giving a definition of happiness that is different than what one normally considers it to be. Many people think that you are happy when everything is going well, when you don't have any problems. But you are saying that happiness is not that; happiness is the ability to accept and to transcend our human condition, which is comprised of failures and short-comings.

Exactly. And I would like to make a clear distinction between happiness and an "easy life," a comfortable life. If we believe that happiness means not having big problems, then we are victims of the temptation of indifference. Being happy means overcoming remorse and bad faith. In fact, there is another dimension to happiness. You are hap-

py when you make others happy. If we keep our "happiness" to ourselves, that is not a Christian happiness. Our
Lord was happy and He commanded us to always live in
joy (1 Th 5:16). But that joy comes to us directly from God
and does not depend on material or historical circumstances.

It is not about escaping our responsibilities, our com-
mitments or our suffering. On the contrary, happiness is
born of the voluntary acceptance of suffering for the joy of
others.

*Thus, one can be happy even in difficult moments, even in
suffering, in the diaspora, genocide…*

Yes. If you read the life of the martyrs, you see that even
when they endured unbearable torture, they were happy,
they didn't abandon their faith. Such was the case of an
Armenian saint of the fifth century: his persecutors
attached his limbs to vices that broke his bones. "Deny the
Christian faith," they said to him. And his retort: "My
bones are answering you." What spiritual strength! If he
had not been in a state of spiritual happiness, he couldn't
have not denied his faith. For the human condition, voluntarily assuming suffering does not exclude the possibility
of joy. If you assume suffering in the name of values to
which you have dedicated your life—your faith, your
commitment to the Kingdom of God, your love for your
neighbor, your love of your country—the difficulties and
even the persecution cannot take away the feeling of
spiritual happiness that God's presence beside us inspires.

What was the happiest day of your life?

It's not easy to choose. Nevertheless, I would like to mention two days. The first is the day that I gave myself to the service of God, at the age of twenty. I remember the moment I approached the altar on my knees, as the Armenian rite requires. For me, it was the greatest joy; I had the feeling that my being, as an individual, had been transformed, changed to a servant of humanity. It was the greatest day of my life, the greatest joy.

The other day was when Armenia became a free country, independent. I don't mean that in the sense of nationalism... It must be understood in the context of a life dedicated to the service of my people, lived entirely in the diaspora. After so many centuries of submission to other powers, after what we call the "yoke" that weighed on our people, when we did not have a country of our own, led by ourselves, and our Church was subject to the tyranny of Communism and the Soviet system... After all that, Armenia's day of independence was declared, and I experienced a joy that was completely unique, singular. We, the Armenians of the diaspora, were outside of our country—not of our own will, but forced to be separated... That day, I said to myself, "Here is the realization of the dream of my ancestors!" That is why I can say that that day, too, was for me, as an Armenian, the happiest.

And the saddest day?

The saddest day was when we suddenly lost Catholicos Zareh I of Cilicia. When I saw him suffering, struck by a heart attack, at the age of forty-eight, I experienced a feeling of revulsion. I couldn't understand why such a person had to lose his life. He was for me a model before God, a model of sacrifice, of devotion, of goodness. In one week, after his death and his burial, I lost seven kilos... That was, without doubt, the saddest day.

Your Holiness, if Jesus Christ gave you a brief audience today during which you would have the opportunity to ask a single question, to make a single request, what would you ask for?

I would beg Him to visit us more often. And I think that He would answer, "But you know very well that I am with you forever, until the end of the world." Thus, you see, He would reproach me for my request...

CHAPTER II

Karekin the First

An Armenian village in Syria

In your installation speech at Etchmiadzin, you said: "I am a child of the diaspora. I wasn't born in the mother country, but the country was born in me." Where were you born?

I was born in Kessab, a village of Armenians in a rural region of Syria that was rather far from the larger cities, right on the border of Turkey.

An Armenian village in Syria. What is the beginning of that story?

The origin of our village is linked to the exodus of Armenians from the city of Ani, the capital of the kingdom under the Bagratids. In the eleventh century, Ani was invaded by the Seljuks, the Turkish dynasty which, in the eleventh and twelfth centuries, dominated Asia Minor, Iran, Iraq, Syria and Armenia. A large part of the Armenian population left the country and found refuge in

Western regions and in Cilicia. The origins of Kessab and Musa Dagh go back to that time. Musa Dagh, the village closest to Kessab, is well known because of its resistance against the Turks during the First World War and because of Franz Werfel's book, *The Forty Days of Musa Dagh*. They say that even in the eleventh century, Catholicos Gregory the Martyrophile had visited the region of Kessab. It was an entirely Armenian village, up until recently, when other Syrians moved there. But today, the large majority of its inhabitants are Armenian. Thanks to its summer climate, there are many Armenians from Aleppo, Latakia, Damascus, and even Beirut who spend their vacations there.

So the primary language in the village was Armenian?

Not exactly. Rather, they spoke the Armenian dialect of Kessab. They taught Armenian literature at school, but at home and in the street, they spoke our dialect, which is quite different than the contemporary literary language.

Your ancestors established themselves in Cilicia in the eleventh century. Then the Armenian kingdom of Cilicia had a rather unusual fate...

Yes. Cilicia was first a principality, then a kingdom. That lasted from 1080 until 1375. The Armenians of Cilicia had strong ties with the Crusaders, and, thanks to that relationship, we have a long history of relations with the West.

In 1375, the capital, Sis, was pillaged...

That's right. Cilician Armenia was invaded by the Mamelukes, who destroyed the kingdom and scattered the
Armenian population. Those refugees gave birth to the
diaspora in the countries of Western Europe, Romania,
Bulgaria, Poland, Hungary, etc. But a substantial Armenian community stayed in Cilicia anyway, where there
was a Catholicossate from 1441 to 1920. With the genocide
of 1915, Armenians were deported from Cilicia, and many
of them were executed in the desert, on the path to exile.
In 1918, after the armistice, those who survived returned to
Cilicia and reestablished their lives in the territory under a
French mandate. But in 1921, when the French evacuated
Cilicia after an agreement with Atatürk, the Armenians, no
longer having any protection, left the country for Syria,
Lebanon and elsewhere. The inhabitants of my village
never left it, since the country became a part of Syria.

*So your ancestors have always lived in that country, since the
eleventh century?*

It's a historical hypothesis, even though there is no historically concrete testimony concerning the origins of Kessab.
But since the dialect is so close to Classical Armenian, it is
extremely probable that their presence goes back to the
eleventh century. Our apostolic Armenian Church is there
with the people, since throughout our history, the Church
has served its people wherever it may be.

Childhood in the village

Let's move on to your family. What is the background of your family?

From the economic point of view, my family had a modest home. Until the age of thirteen, I did not know that electricity existed. What I saw as a child was the realm of village life, with the earth, agriculture, school, and church, which was truly the center of the village: the clock regulated the rhythm of life for everyone. Our house was right next to the church, and there was only a small alley that separated them. So my closeness to the Church in my youth wasn't only spiritual...

My grandfather was a cobbler. My father didn't have a trade of his own and changed jobs several times. In the village, he was the driver for the German mission's orphanage, the "Mission Orient," founded by the great philanthropist Dr. Johannes Lepsius. Then he worked in our village club as well as in Tripoli and in Lebanon. My maternal grandparents were farmers. They did not have a lot of land, but my grandfather worked hard and made a living.

In a sermon at New Jersey's Princeton University, while explaining Jesus' sentence on old water-skins and new wine, you said that you were very familiar with and had used the water-skins of your grandfather... What remains of that village childhood for you?

A connection to the earth. Having participated as a child in the work of the fields and our garden, I "felt" the earth in my existence. I saw how you get the earth, through your work, which is indispensable to us for our lives. Everything that we ate in my family came from the earth, the result of our efforts, of our labor. That taught me the importance of work, by making me understand the words of the Bible: "It is with the sweat of your face that you will eat bread" (Gn 3:19). Moreover, my conviction is that the earth is God's gift. Modern culture has made us lose sight of this, but my childhood in the countryside, with the sowing period and the harvest, made me feel that God is with us through His gifts.

My grandmother, who was very pious, taught us about the existence of God through her life and her prayers, but also through her approach to God's gift. The fact that creation is sacred because it comes to us from God, that's not something I learned in a theology course; whenever a breadcrumb would fall to the ground, grandma would say to us, "Pick it up, it's a gift from God!" And we would pick up, clean off and eat that crumb of bread, since we could not disdain the gift of God. That is why I regret so many attitudes of our culture of consumption. Country life taught me that nature is a precious gift and that men must honor and respect it.

Secondly, we didn't have television, and not even a radio. Everything revolved around the family. Outside of the family, there were three different centers for us: church, school and the Armenian club, which included a library. My love of books began in that club's library, whose first catalog I prepared at the age of fourteen.

Your childhood love of books has marked you; you subsequently wrote a book on books…

Yes, its title is *The Philosophy of the Book*, and it concerns man, especially the Armenian, in relation to books. It is a collection of speeches I delivered during the period of the Lebanese crisis. Each year, in the month of October, we would organize an "exhibition of the Armenian book," with thousands of participants. At the inaugural cere- monies in Antelias, I gave a speech on such or such aspect of the value of the book and the importance of reading.

A patriarchal family

We will return to the theme of the book in Armenian culture. But for now, I would like to continue discussing your childhood. Were you the only child in your family?

No, I have a brother and a sister. I'm the eldest.

Was being the oldest important to your childhood?

Yes, in a certain sense. When my father was away at work, I considered myself responsible for the family. Now, when I look back on my life, I think that my sense of responsibility was strengthened by that experience. When my father was working far from the village, he sent us his salary through the mail. I remember that once, as I was signing the postal order to cash it, the head of the post office said to me, "You are now the person responsible for your family, since it is you who is signing." I was thirteen.

What was your relationship with your parents?

I loved them very much, and they loved me, as well as their other two children. My family was a very safe environment. We didn't know any particularly difficult times. From the material point of view, it was difficult; we never lived with abundance. But my father worked hard, and my mother did all that she could so that we wouldn't lack anything; she loved us so much that she made up for anything we lacked materially. Then there were our grandparents, uncles and aunts, cousins... It was a patriarchal family. We got together often, we all lived in the same neighborhood. The immediate family was inscribed within the extended one. It was in that simple and safe environment that we grew up.

Of your mother and your father, who influenced your childhood more?

I think that both of them influenced me, but they left two different impressions. My father gave me a sense of dignity, of rectitude, of fidelity to moral principles and to the homeland. He was devoted to Armenia's independence movement; when I was still a teenager, he had participated in the struggle of liberation against the Turks. He was a model to us.

My mother was devoted to our family, to us. The affection she showed us and the care she took for our home were exemplary. Like her mother, she was very devout and every day, she would send us to church in the morning and in the evening. She taught me kindness and magnanimity, the attitude of never thinking ill of others. Obviously, as children, we took some liberties; we weren't always well behaved, like all children. Mother often went to church, my father not so much. But every Sunday morning, without exception, they recited the liturgical chants together at home. We, the children, were still in bed.

The mother of a patriarch

Today, your mother is ninety-four years old. She spends a good part of the year here with you, at Etchmiadzin. Did she often accompany you during all your years of service in the different countries of the world?

No, unfortunately, that was not the case. Even when my parents were still living in Lebanon and I was a priest in the Catholicossate in Antelias, in Beirut, I was so busy with my duties that I could rarely see them. My mother felt deprived of my closeness, although she knew that I loved her very much. Then they moved together (my parents, my brother, my sister) to Canada and it was even more difficult for me to see them. So for many years, Mother suffered because of my absence. Presently, they still live in Canada; my father passed away fifteen years ago. My mother spends half the year with me; after so many years, I see that she is still the same person, the one that raised me when I was a child. Moreover, she has continued to treat me the same way. She even remakes my bed...

What is it like for a mother to have a son who is a Patriarch?

I think that it is not a big deal for her. She doesn't brag and is always simple and modest. Surely she recognizes that I have duties, and in some way she's proud of it, saying that God has blessed her in me... But I will always be her child. When I work a lot, she worries; she's happy if I rest; when I am gone, she is not happy.

"He won't make a career of it"

What kind of child were you: open with other children, sociable or shy, reserved?

I was not really shy, but not too involved with the other children, either. I had a lot of friends, companions at school and at the club, but I always kept a certain distance, and I was not bold. When I entered the seminary, one day the dean said to my father: "Your son is intelligent and diligent in his studies, but he is too shy. I do not think that he will have important responsibilities in his life because he is not very daring."

He really didn't have the gift of seeing the future! So your childhood was peaceful, was situated in the countryside in a safe and simple environment. How was your adolescence, that period which is so often difficult, when the child becomes a man?

Adolescence for me was a time of great discovery in terms of my studies. I was completely taken by my reading and school. Also, during vacations, I had an apprenticeship at the tailor's who was a member of our church choir and I often worked in the fields with Grandfather. So, all my

A home or a residence?

What did you learn in your family?

I had a very human education. Moral principles were not something that was taught to us through lessons; they were lived in everyday life, embodied in the framework of everyday family life. My parents really didn't talk to us about honesty or about the love of one's work; it was their example that taught us those things, and the spiritual and moral environment in which we grew up. The moral crisis of today is due to the fact that the family has lost the character of being a home; it has become no more than a simple residence.

The religious education that you received, comprised of your closeness to the Armenian Church, of fidelity to the morals and traditions of your ancestors, was it a veritable handing down of the faith, or rather a part of the national culture, a guarantee of your Armenianness?

I strongly believe that it was above all a handing down of the faith, consisting of the example of those around me, as I already said. But I do not think that you can make a very clear distinction. Armenianness, that feeling of belonging to our people, that national identity, is linked inseparably to our religious faith, since our culture is full of Christianity, and our history was formed by the Christian faith. Today, we talk a great deal about enculturation: the Christian faith must be embodied in the forms of a particular culture. I think that that was the case for Armenia.

When one speaks of the culture of our people, of its thousand-year history, then one necessarily speaks of the Church, of Saint Gregory, of Saint Mesrob Mashtots, who invented the alphabet. I think we will return to the theme of enculturation later, but here, I would like to say that for me, from an existential perspective, it is impossible to conceive of my Armenianness without considering my religious faith.

"Enter and think!"

You entered the seminary rather early, while still an adolescent, at the age of fourteen. Were you affected by the lack of a family environment, of a home?

In the beginning of my studies at the seminary, I suffered from being far from my family; but little by little, it became that home to me. As I entered the seminary, I was struck by the inscription on the gate: *"Khorhé yev medir,"* which means "Think and enter." At that age, I could not really think, in a responsible way, about the vocation, but I entered. Then, obviously, I thought a lot about the vocation, but that reflection developed in the spiritual and intellectual environment of the seminary.

Not yet having the precise idea of the vocation, what made you enter the seminary? The possibility of pursuing your studies? The desire to be in an Armenian context?

I must admit that above all it was the desire to study. In my village, there were not so many possibilities for my future; we did not have a secondary school. So I had begun my apprenticeship with the tailor, since I wanted to help my father with the very modest economic conditions in which we were living. But it was then that Father Movses (Moses) offered me the possibility of going to the seminary. He told me that after my studies, they would ask me if I wanted to become a priest or not; in fact, my desire to become a priest was not something that anyone could have predicted. The idea of the vocation developed slowly inside of me, during my six years in the seminary, where, first, I completed my secondary studies, then theology, philosophy, and Armenology. As the idea developed, prayer and my participation in liturgical life had a very important influence on me, as well as a more profound look at the Christian tradition, of biblical and patristic literature. The spiritual values, which, in the beginning, I was unable to grasp through reason, penetrated my being, were interiorized, assumed.

Which subjects did you like the most? Were there any particular philosophers or theologians who influenced you?

I liked dogmatic theology because it attempted to show, in simple, human language, Christian truths as clearly as possible. I really liked the history of the Church, where you found those same truths, but in real life, transformed into real life throughout history. It was not about memorizing dates or names, but seeing faith actualized in time.

I was most excited about the Fathers of the Church. I remember that once I asked my teacher if I could write an essay on Saint Augustine. The *Confessions*, the *City of God* and all of his writings were for me a very strong call. I wrote ninety pages! I liked the Eastern Fathers, as well: Saint Athanasius, Saint John Chrysostom. I found in them a representation of Christian faith that was not only an intellectual speculation, but rather a preaching, a concrete transmission of spiritual life. Then, while pursuing my studies at the University, I appreciated the difference between the scholastic and the patristic even more. The latter was motivated above all by the concern of the people of God, believers. All the Fathers of the Church were pastors; thus, when they were "doing theology," as people say today, it was done as the communication of the truth and not as an abstract science, detached from real life.

The Fathers of my Armenian Church truly inspired and excited me, particularly those from our Golden Age, the fifth century, when the Sacred Writings were translated into Armenian, as well as the Fathers from the Silver Age (the twelfth century), and the theological school of Armash in Turkey (fourteenth century). As for my teachers and their contribution to my spiritual and intellectual formation, I owe a lot to Shahan Berberian, a philosopher and former student at the Sorbonne, who had taken courses with Henri Bergson. He was a breath of fresh air, elevating our comprehension of the value of human life.

You mentioned the difference between academic theology and the pastoral theology of the Fathers; as a theologian, with which of these two do you identify?

Unquestionably, with the pastoral direction of the Fathers. I have always tried to follow that line, to not be lost in concepts, but to always emphasize the relationship between the truth and the men's lives. My deepest conviction is that the Christian faith is an embodied one, which I tried to show in the introduction of my book, *In Search of Spiritual Life*.

A monk at age twenty

In 1952, at the age of twenty, you took your monastic vows. Is it reasonable to become a monk at the age of twenty?

I do not know if it is reasonable; for me, it was an existential act. I believe I have always been inclined to monastic life, and at the age of twenty, I had no reservations. My desire to serve our Church was so strong that I could not imagine another path for my life than to be a priest. I think it was my work in the seminary that, in addition to making me more knowledgeable, gave me motivation and an inclination towards commitment. Besides, from my understanding, that is the task of every seminary — which is exactly what distinguished it from a College of Theology.

So your task was clear in the priesthood, to be in the service of the Church. But in the Armenian Church, as in all Eastern churches, you also have married clergymen. That said, the choice of monastic life is something very specific in this particular case of service to the Church.

According to our tradition, the monastic vocation does not mean that you must keep a distance from the people. For us, the monasticism is a synthesis of contemplative and active aspects of life. We did not have anchorites as in ancient Egyptian tradition; most Armenians have followed the example of Saint Basil, who balanced prayer and contemplative life with reading and studies, as well as with service to others. Since my adolescence, I felt a strong call toward that type of life. But I have never seen monastic life as a detachment from social life, a distancing from the everyday reality of other people.

Nevertheless, there is the aspect of renouncing a family, marriage, children.

You see, starting in the last year of my studies, I was already teaching in the seminary. But I was so absorbed by my studies, so completely involved in teaching, and so excited to be serving the Church that the question of family was never very important. Also, I was so naturally drawn to this total commitment, in which there were no limits, no obstacles due to family life. It was a sort of spiritual, intellectual enthusiasm that overtook me completely. So I have simply never considered anything else. I could even say that there was a limitless zeal guiding my youth —a zeal that, today, in my old age, surprises me!

Alone, but not lonely

But enthusiasm can often diminish with time. You had no reservations in the beginning; has that certainty remained intact? Haven't you ever known any obstacles or ever wanted to go back in time?

I have had personal difficulties, psychological and otherwise, but I have never seriously thought about going back in time; my total commitment was so strong that the need for a family wasn't as strong as you might think. In terms of the sacerdotal celibacy, if a person is fully dedicated, active and devoted, any other needs, even if they remain, are not obstacles. That is what guided me through my years as a monk.

Apart from those "needs" of human nature, in other words, the question of temptation, haven't you ever desired the company of someone who could offer support, the presence of a someone next to you with whom you could share your happiness or sadness, whom you could always count on in difficult times?

When I was teaching at the seminary, I considered my colleagues and students to be my family; it was the same thing with the people I served as a priest or as a bishop. Besides, I have always had friends on whom I can depend, people whom I could always ask for advice if I had a problem. As for the rest, I have tried to keep a sort of solitude; it is something that has become second nature to me. Often my friends tell me that in spite of my commitment to others, I am still lonely. I would say that I am alone, but not lonely or isolated. Here is my recipe for monastic life: full social engagement, but in keeping room for yourself; and also, having friends with whom you can share your joys as well as your troubles.

At Oxford, with Armenia on his shoulders

From 1957 to 1959 you completed your studies at Oxford. What was that first meeting with the Western, English world like for a young Armenian who had always lived in Lebanon?

My first impression of the students at the Anglican college where I lived was that the people weren't interested in each other. I mean that my first days at Oxford, I was completely alone, and when I sought contact with others, I had a great shock, which I will never forget. I introduced myself to a Scottish student as "Father Sarkissian of the Armenian Church." And his reply was: "Where is Armenia?" That question stunned me. All of a sudden I realized that if people at Oxford did not know where Armenia was, then elsewhere, people probably didn't know very much about it... So I became very determined to make Christian Armenia known as authentically and to as many people as I could. It was a sort of defiance; in me, the English had to see my country, my people, my Church, and I could not disappoint them... It was as if I was carrying all of Armenia on my shoulders!

It gave me an incredible amount of energy. I had to take courses, learn Greek and Latin and write my thesis in two years! Today, I think that if I succeeded, it was thanks to the responsibility I felt and—who knows?—maybe it was thanks to the naive question of that young Scottish student!

What did Oxford and Western culture offer you in terms of your intellectual formation?

Oxford offered me a *challenge,* as the English say; it was the challenge of being true to my identity and to the heart of the universal Christian tradition. Faced with the great Western theological science that I encountered at Oxford, I wondered how what I saw could help us understand and develop the identity of Armenian tradition.

People often look at our Eastern churches as being churches from the past that have maintained an ancient, secular tradition, but that are limited to liturgical life and are what is left of an ancient, glorious era. But while studying Christian history and thought more closely, and having the chance to make comparisons and to see many aspects of our Christian Armenian culture more clearly, I realized that it is by no means a vestige of the past; it never became stagnant as some people believe. I have discovered, for example, that the missionary vocation and our efforts to spread the Gospel have always been present in our tradition, although they had been emphasized less because of certain historical circumstances. But it is necessary to study our Fathers more closely, to rediscover our spiritual heritage. Oxford — which for me meant contact with the Anglican, Catholic, Protestant and Orthodox traditions — truly taught me the significance of my studies: to rediscover and reevaluate the latent forces in the Christian Armenian tradition.

Child prodigy

You entered the seminary at the age of fourteen; at twenty you were a monk and a priest, at thirty-two a bishop, and at forty-five, Catholicos of Cilicia. One might say that you were a child prodigy! You were entrusted with many responsibilities at a

very early age, and your "ecclesiastical career" moved quickly.
Haven't you ever been tempted by "careerism"?

I think I can honestly say no. First of all, I have never
asked for nor tried to obtain a particular function in the
Church. The responsibilities that I have had were entrusted to me by the Church, by my superiors, who might have
appreciated my dedication. They were the people who invited me, and sometimes even forced me, to accept this or
that responsibility.

Secondly, I have always hated the idea of careerism
because it goes against the idea of the calling. You cannot
serve joyfully if you are driven or motivated by concerns
of position or prestige, of love for power, and not by an
interior, spiritual need. Formalism and opportunism, the
arms of any careerist, are foreign to my way of thinking.
The fundamentals of my commitment to the service of God
and my people have been simplicity and hard work.

Bishop

You were made a bishop in 1964. From 1971 to 1973 you were
the bishop of Iran...

Actually, I was the bishop of the south of the country,
since New Julfa, which is close to Isfahan, is actually the
headquarters of the Armenian bishop of the South of Iran.
In the seventeenth century, Isfahan was the capital of the
Safavid dynasty, built by Shah Abbas, who had convinced
more than a thousand Armenians to leave their native land
and to move to Persia to work on the construction of his
palaces and magnificent architectural works, and to parti-

cipate in its commerce. That's why New Julfa was, at that time, the spiritual center of the Armenian people of Iran as well as the episcopal center of the Far East. Armenians living in India, Indonesia, Singapore and other Eastern countries were all part of that diocese.

When Teheran became the capital, the archbishopric moved there; New Julfa remained a cultural center, possessing a remarkable collection of seven hundred manuscripts, a museum, etc. So, outside of my pastoral ministry serving the Armenians of the southern regions of Iran, I was very concerned with our precious cultural heritage.

In 1973, you left Iran and for four years, you were a bishop in New York. I imagine that in America, you were surrounded mostly by Armenians. Nevertheless, the change from Iran to the United States must have been rather abrupt.

First, I must say that American life was not foreign to me; the Anglo-Saxon tradition that I had become acquainted with in England had given me an idea of how life would be in America. Besides, during the years that I was active in the ecumenical movement, at the World Council of Churches, I had met many American theologians, and when I was a bishop in Iran, I had traveled to America to develop our relations.

So in 1973, when I was named bishop in New York, I wasn't completely ignorant of American life; I can even say that I had a certain familiarity with it. So that change from Iran to America was not as traumatizing as one might think. As an Armenian bishop, I have, for the most part, shared the lives of the followers of the Armenian Church in the United States; but I have also kept abreast of the American ecclesiastical milieu, like the National Council of Churches of the U.S.A., as well as of other ecumenical, Catholic, Orthodox and Protestant circles.

Catholicos of Cilicia

From 1977 until your election as Catholicos of All Armenians in Etchmiadzin, you lived in Lebanon, where you were first the coadjutor of the Catholicos and then, after 1983, Catholicos of Cilicia...

I would like to make something clear here. The word "coadjutor" does not indicate a position different from that of the Catholicos; in the Latin and Western conception, a coadjutor is an assistant to the bishop. For us, that is not the case; I was elected by the same process as the Catholicos and I had all the responsibilities of the Catholicos. The Armenian expression *"catholicos atoraguits"* means that he shares the position with the other Catholicos, who is retired or unable to exercise his power for health reasons; in English, one might say *acting Catholicos*. That means that I did not assume the responsibility of the Catholicos after the death of my predecessor, but during the last six years of his life.

In the 1970s and 1980s, while you were living there as the Catholicos of Cilicia, the Near East, that cultural and religious center, was troubled by war. Lebanon in particular was almost in a perpetual state of civil war from 1975. What did the war mean to your ministry?

For fifteen of the eighteen years that I was Catholicos in Lebanon, there was war. My duty, then, was above all to inspire hope in those people who were in despair and in danger of death. So I gave more importance to preaching, to speaking words of hope. In addition to preaching, we proved our faith by constructing buildings for the Church in spite of the ravages of war. We erected at least seven or eight buildings in that time because we never lost hope for Lebanon. Also, I tried to develop the Seminary, the formation of the clergy and the cultural activities of the Catholicossate. In addition to our exhibitions, we tried to develop the editions we had, and to modernize our press, which had become one of the busiest presses of all the diaspora. In short, in Lebanon—for us, the most lively center of the Armenian diaspora—we maintained all of our religious, educational, social and cultural institutions, in spite of the precarious nature of the situation. Thus we tried to show, through our words and actions, our feeling of hope and attachment to the country.

My country, Lebanon

When you were in Antelias, you wrote a brochure entitled The Cross Made of the Cedars of Lebanon, *which was full of love for that country. What does Lebanon represent to you?*

Lebanon to me is a country that must preserve its unity at any price. As the Catholicos of Cilicia, I felt a great responsibility to unify the Armenian community and to dedicate myself to the cause of a unified Lebanon, a country that has a dialogue between Islam and Christianity. I have always thought that were that dialogue to fall apart, there would be no more Lebanon. Lebanon is synonymous with dialogue, one that is profound and convivial. For the West, dialogue is often no more than an exchange of ideas, so there is the Marxist-Christian dialogue, the interreligious dialogue, ecumenical, and many others. But in the Near East, Christians and Muslims live together, and dialogue is the art of living together, sharing, and not an exchange of ideological ideas.

From that perspective, our community, despite certain pressures, has played the role of a lawyer for the unity of Lebanon. We have suffered a lot because of that role, but we have never strayed from that line of action. Lebanon is a geographically small country, but it has a spiritual richness, a richness of communication, of communion between different religions and cultures. That characteristic must be maintained no matter what. I was very happy when the Pope, during his last visit to Lebanon, continually emphasized that Lebanon must remain the country of understanding and cooperation that it has always been. Personally, I admire the Lebanese for their efforts to maintain that message, which is what Lebanon is for other countries.

What you are saying makes me think of an expression that you once used: "My motherland of Armenia and my country of Lebanon."

That's right.

You were born in Syria, but to an Armenian family; for the greater part of your life, you have lived in Lebanon. Who is Catholicos Karekin I: an Armenian, a Lebanese, or a Syrian?

I would say that he is all three at the same time.

Catholicos of All Armenians at a turning point in history

On April 4, 1995, you were elected the Supreme Patriarch and Catholicos of All Armenians, by the National Ecclesiastical Assembly, composed of more than four hundred delegates from Armenian communities from all over the world. Your new engagement with the Church came at a very particular moment for Armenia, which one could call a historical turning point…

The work of the ministry of the Catholicos of All Armenians, like the ministry of any head of a church, is immense, difficult and full of responsibilities; but the job is probably even more difficult in this time of radical change. Even though I did not live in Armenia before my election, I have always carried my country, whose history has seen so many upheavals, with me in my heart. This historical moment began with Nagorno-Karabagh's liberation movement, which led to the proclamation of our free and independent Republic. There are two great tasks for the Catholicos today. On the one hand, there is the job of repairing all that was destroyed during seventy years of an aggressively atheist regime; on the other hand, there is the job of constructing a new Christian awareness in this free and independent State.

It is much easier to begin building in a place that has nothing than to restore a heritage as deeply wounded as Armenia's. But we must accept the reality of the present situation and clear the way for a renewal, a new enthusiasm. In the time of Communism, all that the Church could do was to preserve and conserve what it had. But today, we must go and meet our people. It is now a question of the apostolate, whose goal is the re-Christianization of our people in the image of what they have always been: a Christian nation who showed its identity with creativity and perseverance—even at the cost of life. The transfiguration of our people is a spiritual, moral, human and cultural formation. A nation cannot stand solely on its economic and political foundations; it must possess a moral tenacity, and the source of that moral education is the Church.

Another fundamental task is to maintain strong links to our diaspora. There are more of our dioceses outside of Armenia than inside. The integrity of the Church must be protected.

There are two principal forms of the modern Armenian language: Eastern Armenian, spoken in contemporary Armenia and Iran, and Western Armenian, spoken in the other communities of the diaspora. Each linguistic group has its own corresponding culture and mentality. From your first visits to your predecessor, Catholicos Vasken I, you have always tried very hard to speak Eastern Armenian here, which offers a pleasant surprise. Nevertheless, the fact that the Catholicos is an Armenian of the diaspora, a "Westerner," must make for some negative reactions among Eastern Armenians.

I don't think so. First, I must say that I had already had some experience with the Eastern Armenian language and culture because I was a bishop in Iran, and I had visited Soviet Armenia several times. Moreover, in our Armeno-logical studies in the West, we read many Eastern writers. Besides, the linguistic difference is not as great as you might think. On the other hand, concerning the difference in mentality, that's something more sensitive; that con-cerns the way in which one behaves or faces problems, and one's methodological approach to work. For that, I try to be as flexible as possible, to be ready to listen to my brothers and to show everyone that I am there to give everything I can to this country and its people. In any case, my responsibility is not limited to the inhabitants of the Republic of Armenia. The communities of the diaspora are included in the expression "Catholicos of *All Armenians*," as I said before.

A Catholicos from Oxford

But a Catholicos with a degree from Oxford, who has lived in several different countries, traveled all over the world, kept ecu-menical contacts, wouldn't he be seen as a foreigner to a parish priest in a little Armenian village who has never left his country, who never had the opportunity to pursue theological studies, who might have had problems with the regime...

For me, there is not a great distance between the people here and myself. Yes, I studied at Oxford, but I don't think that that is the most important thing about my life! In any case, that isn't something I always bring up to the people I'm talking to. Rather, I try to identify with people, to speak their language, to be interested in their problems. It's not a strategy; I simply think that if the Apostle Saint Paul made himself Greek with the Greeks and Jewish with the Jews, then I must make myself an Armenian from Armenia with my people.

Moreover, having been born and raised in a rural setting, I think I have always carried the experience of a simple life within me. I feel a great affinity with the simplest segments of the population.

Do you get support from your bishops, the clergy, the people? And do you think that you understand the problems of post-Soviet Armenia, having never lived in the USSR?

I think they support me, for the most part. As for my understanding of our post-Soviet society, that actually is not so easy. Armenia has inherited certain typical problems of post-Soviet life, but our society is changing rapidly. The same problems exist in the other countries of the former Soviet Union, where we have Armenian communities: Russia, Georgia, the Ukraine, Tadjikistan and Kazakhstan, and even in the Baltic nations. Since I did not live here during Communism, I have some trouble understanding certain phenomena that persist today. That is why I am always ready to listen to my advisors. It seems to me that with their help, and with the help of God, I already understand those problems much better than I did before.

The Church in a state of movement

You are a very active man. If one spends a few days here, as I have, one cannot help but be surprised by your busy schedule, by the fact that you are always receiving bishops, priests, government officials, pilgrims, etc. Moreover, you travel a lot in order to consecrate new churches, to visit different dioceses. You also travel abroad to visit the Armenians of the diaspora, to see other Christians, to participate in ecumenical conferences. In a word, as a pastor, you preach a lot; you speak on state television, on the radio, you write books. It seems that the fact that you are so active has surprise people here in Armenia. Some people think that such a level of activism could diminish the dignity of the Catholicos...

It seems to me that that impression is rather superficial. Above all, a pastor must be with his people. The idea that the Catholicos is distanced from his people belongs to the past, to the time when there were not as many possibilities for transportation, nor the challenges faced by the Church today. In the time of the Soviet domination, the Catholicos was forced to not be with the people, and to not show himself publicly. It was forbidden by the authorities. That is why my predecessor traveled more in the diaspora than he did within the country.

On this matter, I would like to give you a very eloquent example. When, in April 1989, I had to come to Armenia as the Catholicos of Cilicia at the invitation of my predecessor, I wrote to him that I would like to visit the monastery of Datev, one of the most remarkable theological centers in the history of our Church. The very night that I arrived, Catholicos Vasken said to me, "When I received your letter, I was very moved and I realized that in the thirty-three years that I have been Catholicos, I have never visited the monastery of Datev. Now you have come for a few days from Cilicia, and if you go there, what will they say? Where is our Catholicos? So I have decided that we will go together." So we visited all of the south of Armenia together. And before thousands of followers, he said the following: "Dear followers, you know very well that I have never paid you a visit. I do not know if I did the right thing or not... Certainly, if I had come before, you would not have been able to receive me publicly." It was 1989 and there were dioceses that he had not been to since his election in 1955. Today, when I go to the many places in the south and north of the country, people say, "We have never seen the Catholicos..." But I repeat, time and again, that he could not have done differently.

For a long time, it was the same thing for the Popes—they did not move. But you know well that everything changed with Pope Paul VI. I think that now we are seeing the evangelical aspect of the pastor. The Catholicos is not some legend, but a servant who must go to the people, as Christ did, as the Fathers of the Church did. We must free ourselves from the legacy of the Middle Ages. The Church is not a fixed institution; today, it must be above all in a state of movement.

Before your election as the Catholicos of All Armenians, you were a citizen of Lebanon. When did you visit Armenia for the first time?

In 1966, then in 1968 and 1969. Then I could not return to Armenia until 1988, when I came immediately after the earthquake to show my solidarity and to offer my cooperation to Catholicos Vasken. Between that time and my election, I returned five times.

Was it difficult for a foreign hierarch of the Armenian Church to visit Soviet Armenia?

If the hierarch was seen in a favorable manner by the Communist regime, then there weren't any difficulties; but if he was known to be anti-communist, then that was another story. In any case, when someone came here, he could speak publicly only if he praised the government. You know that starting in the 1950s until the end of the regime, that political situation caused a controversy between the two Catholicossates. For the Soviet State I was *persona non grata*, since as Catholicos of Cilicia I was part of the opposition to the regime, and I was known as an anti-communist. My absence of almost twenty years was due to those political reasons, and not due to the conflict between the two Catholicossates. The three times that I was here during the Soviet regime, I was the representative of the See of Cilicia for some conversations with the Holy See of Etchmiadzin. Already at that time I had a good personal relationship with Catholicos Vasken.

Toward the land of his fathers

You have lived almost all of your life away from your historical homeland, and at the age of sixty-three, you arrived in the land of your fathers. The fact of living your life in the service of a country to which it was difficult for you to travel makes me think of the destinies of the Old Testament patriarchs, such as Moses or Abraham. What does Armenianness mean to an Armenian of the diaspora?

I believe that it is first necessary to say that our dispersion is not a free choice; it was imposed upon us. When you live far from your homeland, you always feel nostalgia for it. In today's diaspora, there is a new generation for whom the country of their ancestors is not as familiar as it was for their parents or grandparents. For example, the young Armenians in France, in other European countries or in the United States did not grow up in the Armenian language or culture as we did in the Near East. They are third- or fourth-generation Armenians, who are well integrated in the countries where they live. Those young people are aware that their origins are here, in Armenia, but from an emotional point of view, they don't feel connected in an existential way, so to speak.

For our generation, it was different; for us, Armenia was always present and lived in our spirits. The traumatizing experience of the genocide was present throughout our generation, and in 1965 we saw the fiftieth anniversary of that episode. Over the years, we became indignant because of the indifference of the world to the Armenian cause. We saw the births of many different states in Africa and Asia, and we always proclaimed our desire for an independent state of our own. Today, our dream has come true.

Also, with the creation of our free and independent state, a psychological change is underway in our people, both here and in the diaspora. Now that Armenia is the responsibility of Armenians, and that we are enjoying all liberties, there is a new awareness of our identity, of our role in the world. That awareness has given us back our national dignity. Thus, the youth of the diaspora who come here, in spite of the very difficult economic conditions of our Republic, are proud to see a free country. So it seems to me that the sense of belonging to our country is developing even more, both here and in the diaspora.

One of the works from early Christian literature, the Letter to Diogenetus, *contains a passage describing Christians in terms that seem appropriate to the situation of a diaspora: "Christians all live in their own homeland, but as foreign citizens. All foreign lands are homelands to them, and all homelands are foreign..."*

In my opinion, there is only an apparent resemblance there. In the countries where our people of the diaspora live, we do not have that feeling of being foreign that the first Christians had while waiting for the *Parousia*. The Armenians of the diaspora truly belong to the countries where they were born and where they live; but they do not belong exclusively to those countries, since, at the very time that they are integrated and engaged in the social life of that country, they are also aware that they belong to another country, that of their ancestors, which we like to call the "mother homeland." Armenia is our country of origin and that awareness is normally quite strong in Armenians. There is no contradiction in that double belonging.

There were moments in our history when that feeling of a promised land was very strong. However, it's not so much a question of a promised land, but an acquired land, and not only today, since a certain number of Armenians have always lived here—just as, for example, the Jewish people were entirely exiled to Egypt. We have known exile very well, with the diaspora, but that has never affected the unity of the nation.

Purifying one's Armenianness

You have lived in several countries: Syria, Lebanon, England, Iran, the United States, Armenia. What did those peoples and cultures offer you?

A richness of diversity; like a mosaic whose different colors are in harmony, and it is precisely harmony that creates beauty. Or also like a symphony in which the melodies of different instruments work together to create a unity. All the cultures that I have known in my life have enriched me, on a human level, and I would say have helped me to "purify my humanity." What I mean by that is, while being very close to my country, I have never been an exclusive nationalist, thanks to the help I received from the cultures and the people among whom I have lived. That is why I am very convinced that contact between nations and cultures is always positive. The greatest civilizations were born at cultural crossroads, and they are the result of the meeting of different cultures. The "dialogue between cultures" that people talk about so frequently today constitutes the path toward peace and the well-being of humanity.

I think that if there is a difference between the beginning and the end of our century, it's that today we must have a clear awareness of the fact that war and isolation lead nowhere, and that peace, understanding, and cooperation are the key to happiness. Human values are never contained within a single culture; such an absolutization would lead to catastrophe. I think that to truly feel one's affiliation to a country, and its uniqueness, requires an acceptance of others and their sense of affiliation to their own countries. On the other hand, when you accept the culture of the other, you can and must remain faithful to your own identity. We find an example of that in Christ Himself, who belonged completely to the Jewish culture of His time.

I would say that in the history of Armenia, there has always been an openness to other cultures. Our "Golden Age" in the fifth century begins with our meeting with the Greek and Syriac cultures.

To answer your question, I would say that my multicultural experience has enriched me as a person and has purified me as an Armenian.

Your country has a unique charm for the visitor, due to its history, its thousand-year-old culture, etc. But Armenia has had a destiny full of suffering and difficulties. If you had the chance to choose, not a passport, but a cultural, historical nationality — you who have lived in several different countries and have known so many cultures — which would you choose?

I would choose my identity. I cannot imagine any other possibility for me than that of being faithful to my Armenian culture, so full of the Christian faith. I do not disparage any of the other cultures that I have known, but my nationality is something that I cannot separate from myself, not even as an abstraction.

But I would like to add something. I often think about our humanity, about its richness, and its harmonious diversity. What beauty God gave us, giving us life on this planet, which is like a garden with so many different kinds of trees! If the trees were all the same, there would be no beauty. For me, being Armenian only has meaning if I am in contact, and I would like to say, *in communion* with other nations. It is from this perspective that I hope the third millennium will have more of an awareness of the unity of nations, unity in diversity but without oppositions, without the tensions that are often provoked by political considerations that are too narrow.

CHAPTER III

Faith

A question of life

Your Holiness, why do you believe?

I have never asked myself that question because I feel that I believe, and I could not *not* believe; simply put, my faith was born in me during my childhood, and over time, it has become even deeper, more integrated into the framework of my life. To ask me that question, then, would be like asking why I exist. The presence of faith is such an existential fact for me that I cannot give you an answer that is purely logical or by reasoning intellectually. Faith is a gift of God, something inherent to my existence. It's a question of life, and not of reason or of conviction, which is why I don't really know how to answer that question!

So you are saying: I believe in the same way that I breathe or that my heart beats…

Yes.

But how does believing change a man's life?   At the European Ecumenical Assembly of Graz, you spoke of the difference, of the distinctiveness of the Christian in relation to other men.   What did you mean by that?

Each faith has a context.   For me, the context of what I believe is Christianity.   But the Christian faith, not being a philosophy, must be concretely expressed in my life, in my service, in my work.

What I was saying in Graz is that we, Christians, have frequently become formalists; our Christianity is sometimes no more than formal.   The authenticity of our faith and its dynamism is often lacking because we belong also to a secular culture.   So I was saying that we Christians, if we are authentic and faithful to our Christian faith, we must feel that *distinctiveness*, that *difference* from atheists and the non-religious, that is, those who are indifferent to religion.   We respect those people, and we do not exclude them from our love; but we cannot ignore our difference in our experiences, in our ways of living and behaving, of interacting with others.   Because the Christian faith leaves a very distinct impression in all aspects of life.

"You cannot change the color of your skin"

A father of your Church in the fifth century, Saint Yeghishé, in one of the most important historical works of classical Armenian literature, tells the story of the martyrs who died in battle against the Mazdean Persians in AD 451, and quotes the words of the valiant Armenian hero of the battle, Vartan: "The enemy thinks that we wear Christianity as one wears a vest; now he will see that a person cannot change the color of his skin."

That means that faith runs deeply, that it becomes part of us, and at the same time faith is a gift, something that one receives, like the color of your skin...

There is surely a constitutive element of the gift in faith. But that gift is not something that is the prerogative of certain people; it is given to all men, but there are those who are receptive to it, and those who are less receptive. One's life situation determines whether that gift is more or less evident in a person; some people do not let it develop in their souls, and let it die. On the other hand, there are those who say that they do not have faith, but then a certain moment, event, meeting, or reading—as was the case for Saint Augustine with *Tolle, lege*—reveals to them the faith that was living in the depths of their heart.

If I understand correctly, you are comparing faith to a talent, like a beautiful voice, or the ability to write well, etc. The person who has that talent might not take notice of it, notice it all of a sudden, develop it, or let it go, not use it. But if you do not have that talent, you cannot give it to yourself. The expression of Saint Yeghishé can also be understood in that manner: One cannot appropriate faith, as one cannot change the color of one's skin...

In speaking of gifts, I am not alluding to talents, which are the particular gifts of a person. I said that faith is given to us, and we have many universal gifts, which are part of our humanity, like sight, hearing, or the ability to breathe. Faith is not a particular color of our lives, like a talent, but rather the canvas on which these colors are expressed.

That gift is for all men and women, since it is inherent to our humanity. Every person can either refuse it or welcome it and bear witness to it, since what Christians call "faith" is neither an intellectual education, nor an esoteric doctrine, but an acting, operating force.

So you believe that every man is born with the gift of faith?

Yes, I think so.

You have said that a person can be more or less receptive to this gift. What can one do to welcome and cultivate the gift of faith? Many people say they seek God without succeeding in finding Him.

I think that those people should start with the idea that reason is not all that man is. We have reason to apply it to earthly life, in our condition as humans. But man transcends reason. Pascal said: "The heart has reasons that reason doesn't know." There is a sixth sense in us. I would like to return to the comparison I made just now between faith and hearing or sight. I know very well that some people are lacking in one or more of those senses, and are not lessened in their humanity because of it. But faith is the sixth sense that can never be lacking, since it is inherent to human nature. Unfortunately, we often do not use that sense, and try to replace it with reason, whether by denying God or by looking for Him... But our reason cannot fully grasp God, even though it can strengthen that sixth sense, faith.

Faith, reason, and the heart

You are introducing a theme that I was just coming to: that of reason and faith. For some, they are terms in opposition, mutually exclusive. While there are theologians and philosophers who have found God through reason, there are other thinkers, on the contrary, who have distanced themselves from Him through reason.

Is our intellect an obstacle to faith or a tool to help us find it?

I do not think that it is an obstacle. On the contrary, it is a very important element to apply in the life of the gift of faith. There is no one who, in exercising his reason, could succeed in discovering a transcendent reality. Several thinkers in their philosophical systems have felt the necessity of the idea of God and many of them have ended up affirming His existence; but the god of philosophers often has no relation to our lives. There, it is only the idea of God, a notion, and not God Himself. For the believer, God is active in our lives. The difference between the atheist and the believer is precisely this: often, atheists do not reject the idea of the eternal and infinite Being, but for them, God is not a part of their lives, which are guided solely by reason.

So I would say that reason does not contradict faith, but often reason does not accept the intervention of God in human life; that is where faith comes in. It is a question of friendship and communion with God. When I think about God, I do not think of a First Cause of other causes, as Aristotle said. I think of a God who is a creator, and thus love, a God who gives us the secret to happiness. In the Christian faith, God manifests Himself to man as love through His creation, His revelation and the communion that man can establish with Him. Faith shows us a God who touches our lives and not a God who is a category of thought that only has a relation to reasoning.

But why is it so difficult to find God? Why does He not show Himself clearly? Saint Paul saw a light, and heard a voice calling him; but on the other hand, many people who would like to find God never meet Him. Sometimes, people have the impression that the Almighty is a bit shy.

I do not know why God does not show Himself to us as He did to Saint Paul. I know that all men are not Saint Paul... I think that we cannot really ask why God does not do this or that; it is up to Him in His infinite love to decide how He reveals Himself to each person. But there are several ways in which He shows Himself: Creation has clear imprint of God, and many people, in looking at a plant, have found God. Others have found Him while contemplating the development of a human embryo... Naturally, there are particular cases in which God shows Himself more clearly to certain people; but even in those cases, what a variety of manifestations! God did not show Himself in the same way to Saint Paul and to Saint Peter or to Saint Thaddeus. In the Scriptures, He revealed Himself to Moses at Sinai, and He showed Himself as in the person of the only Son, Jesus Christ, and He continues to show Himself in the lives of the saints.

A very obvious manifestation of God for me is in the people who have devoted their lives to His service and to the service of men. I have already spoken about Mother

Theresa; I cannot think of her without seeing in her a reflection, a manifestation of God.

When you look at nature, with its beauty and majesty,
you often feel the presence of God. There are thus different
ways of finding God, and it's our job to listen. But often,
we have lost our sensitivity to the signs of His presence...

*People often say that there is a difference in the way of perceiving
and expressing faith between Christians of the East and of the
West. In general, a Westerner finds faith through reason, while
an Easterner finds it through the heart. For you as an Easterner
who has known the West very well, what is faith for you: something that comes from the intellect or from feelings?*

For me, faith is a fact of life, in which both the heart and
the intellect are involved. I would like to say here that for
Easterners, over the course of centuries, the Christian faith
has been expressed in community life: in the family, in the
work of the fields... In the West, Cartesian thought tends
to divide, to compartmentalize life into different sectors:
the sector of work and business, the sector of private life,
the sector of sports, etc. With that compartmentalization,
faith and religion constitute only one of the quarters, one
of the slices of the individual's life: the religious sector.
Thanks to our less rationalist mentality, in the psychology
of Easterners, those different aspects of life are less clearly
separated, and the Christian faith can permeate man
entirely.

Sometimes in the West, I have had the impression that
family life was only a form of communal residency, in the
same place, of isolated people. What is lost is the common

experiences between members of the same family: meals eaten together, hours of prayer and leisure. The tendency to compartmentalize life undermines the communal dimension of the Christian faith.

The Gospel shows us that in all aspects of His life, Jesus was always the same, and that His faith was involved in all of His activities: when He was preaching, when He was sharing a meal with a family, when He was working on Peter's boat... His Faith was involved in all aspects of His life, and for Him nothing was separated from religion. Thus, for every Christian, faith must enlighten each aspect of his existence; I am not a Christian if my faith is no more than a few prayers at church and does not affect my way of living and working. Religion is not limited to Sundays!

It is obvious that a split between faith and deeds exists in the East as well as in the West; but the conception of life in the West, which compartmentalizes human activities, often encourages that disassociation.

Metanoia

But what is more important: one's deeds or one's faith? Does one save oneself through faith or rather through acts?

I think that there is a dichotomy there that is not justified. Saint James in his epistle (Jas 2:14-25) teaches us that faith is inseparable from deeds: faith without deeds is dead, and deeds without faith have no foundation.

That is why I think that that question, which has occupied the minds of theologians, particularly after the Reformation, is due to the situation of the Church in the

Middle Ages, when deeds were strongly emphasized and living faith was lacking because of a certain institutional-ization and authoritarianism in the Church. That explains why the theology of the time reflects that dichotomy. But faith and deeds are linked inseparably; one cannot keep one's faith without harmonizing his actions with that faith. For me, faith is not a group of convictions that I keep for myself, but something that must emanate from me in my social life. Faith means light, and light must shine.

Today, our "shine" as Christians leaves much to be desired: the believers who show their faith in public life, courageously and consistently, are very few. Too often we are sterile, like trees that don't offer fruit; we must remember that Jesus Christ said that we recognize a tree by its fruit, and that He scorned a sterile fig tree.

One of the concepts that comes up frequently in your sermons is that of metanoia *— conversion, change. You often talk about it in reference to Christians, to those who already believe, who are supposed to already be converted...*

Metanoia is the constant act of purification in human life and the process of elevating oneself toward God. As human beings, we have the possibility of failure — the liberty of failure. We are weak, sinners, imperfect. However, Jesus said to us: "Be perfect as your heavenly Father is perfect." I believe that that means: "Try with all your might to approach perfection, which is God."

I would like to mention here a little story that involves an Armenian saint, John of Nisibis, which is told in a book known under the name Paustos of Byzantium; it's from the fifth century but its contents go back to the fourth. Saint John wanted to climb Mount Ararat to see Noah's Ark. He walked for a long time, climbing arduously, but he never reached the summit. At one point, he was so tired that he stopped to catch his breath and fell asleep. In his slumber, an angel appeared to him and gave him a piece of wood from the Ark, which we have kept among our relics in Etchmiadzin.

Now, I see in this story a metaphor for the human condition: we climb, we try with all our might…and we never achieve the ultimate goal. But the act of *approaching* it is already a victory. *Metanoia* is that constant walk in the purification of oneself — in the improvement of the quality of our service to others. We must walk, even though we know that by our efforts alone, we will never reach the summit, since the summit is God Himself and we are not gods. But God has us participate in His divinity.

Trinity and beauty

For Christians, God is One in three People. In the Trinity, each hypostasis, *each divine Person, is Himself in the extent to which He presents Himself to others. That gift of self and the reception of the other* hypostases *– which is called* perichorese, *interpenetration – does not change the identity of each Person. It is because of that perfect reciprocal gift of the Father, the Son and the Holy Spirit that we believe that God is love.*

Do you think that the Trinity could be a model for social relationships: between men, nations, cultures, churches?

For me, the Trinity is a model for all human behavior. The unity of God is not uniformity, nor is it monolithic. Unity through love requires otherness and distinction, experienced not as antagonism, but as a gift of love and communion, interpenetration. It is there, in that unity, that I find the source of beauty. Beauty is in fact a manifestation of unity, in terms of the harmony of different entities. In that sense, social life is art *par excellence*; being so different, living together would mean reconciling our difference with the awareness of belonging to the same nation, or to humanity. When the balance of unity and diversity is disturbed, we have either conflicts and chaos, or dictatorship.

So I think that the Trinity is the source of every authentic human, social relationship.

Let's continue with art. God is truth: theology seeks to explain that characteristic of God. But God is also beauty; could one consider the vocation of art being rather close to that of theology: explaining and showing God in terms of beauty?

I congratulate you on that formulation, which I like very much. I think that in our theology, which is an heir to academics and sometimes suffocated by a certain intellectualism, we have lost that sense of a relationship between beauty and truth.

When we speak of truth, we're not talking about a logical truth; in Christianity, the truth is not an abstraction, but is always tied to life. Jesus defined Himself as "the way, the truth and the life." It is precisely there where beauty and truth meet. The form of theology of the Fathers of the Church was doxology, a confession of faith that always praised the glory of God. There was the exaltation of God, and at the same time the act of man elevating himself from his earthly condition to find his integrity in the harmony of his spiritual being.

That sense of beauty, that participation in the glory of God, has stayed alive in liturgical life. But art also explains something about God, makes us participants in His life. Recently, I have seen tangible signs of a rediscovery of art in some theological treaties.

If it is true that in their ways of finding the sacred, Westerners follow their intellect, while Easterners follow their hearts, maybe those two groups of Christians are being called to testify together to these two definitions of God, as truth and beauty. And these two approaches are complementary and need each other, since without the support of the spiritual experience of the East, the Western approach runs the risk of becoming a philosophy or a barren doctrine, and the Eastern approach, without the support of Western rationality, could fall into sentimentalism...

I agree. And I think that this could be one of the greatest blessings of ecumenism. If the two traditions want to serve the same Christ, the dialogue and the opening up of one to the other in confidence and love are indispensable. This dialogue of love could be very beneficial to each of the two traditions and for all of Christianity. That would truly be what people have often called "breathing with both lungs."

CHAPTER IV

The Armenian Church

Apostolic origins

Your Holiness, your Church is one of the oldest in the world. According to tradition, Christianity was being preached in your country immediately after the Resurrection and the Ascension, by the apostles Thaddeus and Bartholomew. That said, neither Rome nor Constantinople: you have not inherited your faith from another church, but directly from the apostolic community.

Yes. The origin of the Armenian Church in the age of the apostles, when there were not yet any jurisdictional structures of the churches, is today known to be a historically founded truth. The Christian faith existed in Armenia well before Saint Gregory. According to the oldest tradition, the seeds of Christianity were sown by the apostles whom you just mentioned. After that initial period of the declaration of the Word of God in Armenia, Christian preaching continued through the first three centuries.

Here, I would like to react to the extremely critical approach that certain historians have applied to the question of the origins of our Church. They say that before

Saint Gregory, there was no Christianity in Armenia and that everything we know about the history of the pre-Gregorian period is simply legend. Some even say that the apostolic origin was intentionally invented by our Church in the fifth century (the oldest date to which Armenian sources can be traced) to prove its independence.

I cannot enter into the details of the academic debate here, which, from my point of view, has lost its value and its pertinence, since it was initiated by a confessional polemic. But I would like to briefly summarize the findings of the recent research of historians who worked on the subject of the presence of Christianity in Armenia before Saint Gregory.

First, it is clear that at the foundation of the documents written in the fifth century that we have, there is an oral tradition that is not a work of fiction, but which corresponds to a very precise historical reality, even though the norms of hagiographic literature can be seen in it. There could not be written sources more ancient than that, since the Armenian alphabet was created right in the fifth century.

The oral tradition of the first centuries A.D. — which is seen in the writings of the fifth century — speaks eloquently of Armenian martyrs and missionaries from Eastern Syria (Antioch, Edessa, Nisibis, Melitene) and from Cappadocia. We know that in southern Armenia, before Saint Gregory, there was a Christian center (*Ashtishat*), a Church that was even considered the "mother of all churches" of Armenia, and that fact clearly proves the presence of Christian preaching in our country in the pre-Gregorian period. In the fourth century, the Armenian Church was known as the "Seat of Saint Thaddeus" (*Ator Thadeosi* or *Thadeakan*

Ator) according to the expression of the historian Paustos of Byzantium.

Even if our written Armenian sources did not necessarily date from before the fifth century, we have several other pieces of evidence from non-Armenian historians of the first centuries on the existence of Christianity in Armenia, such as Eusebius of Caesarea (AD 265-340), who in his *History of the Church* talks about a bishop of Armenia named Meroujan, to whom the bishop of Alexandria had addressed a letter. All of this data cannot be considered a fiction or a falsification.

Secondly, it is a universally accepted truth that in the first century, Christianity existed in Cappadocia (already noted in Saint Peter's epistle) and in Eastern Syria, not only in Antioch, but as far as Edesse, Melitene, etc. Since Armenia had so many political, cultural and commercial relations with Cappadocia and Eastern Syria, it is not hard to believe that Christianity was being preached in Armenia as well. It is historically proven that Jewish communities existed in Armenia in the apostolic age, and those communities were the first homes that the apostles and missionaries found for Christian preaching.

Thirdly, it is clear that in order for our King Tiridates to proclaim through his edict that Christianity was the religion of the state in the beginning of the fourth century, there was necessarily a preparation. The decision of a king and the efforts of a single missionary would not have been enough to change the religion of the people in one day, especially since the people were firmly rooted in a pagan tradition that was tied to the Mazdean religion.

That is why we believe that the origins of our church date back to the first century, that they are apostolic, and that that continuity has never been broken.

Gregorian church?

That explains the epithet of your church, which you define as the "Armenian Apostolic Church." However, one often sees the designation "Gregorian church."

That name is fairly recent, and comes from the text of the *Regulation* for the Armenian Church [*Polozhenie* in Russian], approved by Czar Nicholas I in 1836. It is in this document that our church is called Gregorian, which the Armenians have translated with the word *Lousavorchagan* ("those who follow Saint Gregory").

The story of Saint Gregory that has been passed onto us through tradition is very turbulent. His father killed King Tiridates' father. King Tiridates had all of the assassin's family killed except for Gregory, whose escape to Cappadocia was aided by the King's Christian guard. There, Gregory was raised in the faith and baptized. To make up for his father's sin, he entered into the service of King Tiridates, who had been sojourning among the Romans, and returned to Armenia with him. It was only then that the King learned that his servant was Christian and the son of his father's killer. After having him thrown in a pit that served as a prison for criminals condemned to death, where the saint stayed for thirteen years, the King went mad. Finally,

*cured of his madness by Gregory, Tiridates had himself baptized
along with all of his people.*

What is true in this account?

Historians have very different positions concerning this
matter. What I think is that in this tradition, there is a
foundation, a core of historical truth that was presented in
the popular forms of the oral tradition, in accordance with
the canons of the hagiographic genre. Consequently, the
historical framework has undergone some amplification,
some exaggeration, and the information concerning the
miraculous events in his life has played a large part in that.
That is the case for most of the lives of the saints, and for
the stories of the origins of many churches in the world.

*The miracle to which you are alluding is the healing of King
Tiridates?*

Yes. Another miracle is the fact that he was able to survive
thirteen years in that underground prison, or that, according to tradition, a pious woman threw a piece of bread
down to him every day.

*While summarizing the story of Saint Gregory, I mentioned the
detail of his passage from Cappadocia to Rome, before returning
to Armenia. Some see in this detail a link between the nascent
Armenian Church and Rome...*

First of all, from the historical point of view, one cannot
say with certainty that Saint Gregory went from Cappa-

docia to Rome.   In the literature of the time, the name
"Rome" could also refer to Byzantium or to the Eastern
Roman Empire. Saint Gregory joined King Tiridates when
the latter arrived in Armenia to conquer the land of his
"paternal heritage," his father's throne.

Secondly, at that time, there were no relations between
the Christians of Armenia and Rome.   Historically, our
Church had very close relations with Cappadocia and with
Edessa, Nisibis, Melitene and Eastern Syria, and Antioch,
the most important center; so missionaries were coming to
Armenia from these regions. The Church of Cappadocia
had its own identity and was not legally bound to Rome.
However, even though there were not any jurisdictional
ties, they professed the same faith, since there were not yet
any theological disputes or dogmatic divergences.

*Tiridates adopted Christianity in the year 301.   It is worth
noting that that date precedes by twelve years Constantine's
Edict of Milan, which established religious liberty in the Roman
Empire. Since then, you have always been a Christian nation.*

On the subject of the exact date of the adoption of Christianity as the religion of the state, I must make an important
remark. The date 301 that you noted is the traditionally
recognized one. However, some recent studies, in light of
the discovery of historical documents, have established
that the episcopal consecration of Saint Gregory in Cappadocia could not have taken place before 314, since the
archbishop Leontius who presided over that consecration
did not occupy the See of Caesarea before that date. So

they have proposed the year 313 as the date of the adoption of Christianity, which precedes that consecration.

Whatever the case, what is important here is not the date, but the extraordinary event—which remains the first in the history of Christianity.

In any case, the conversion of Armenia was not an event that took place on a specific day or that resulted from a single action, like the king's edict. Rather, it was an evolution, a chain of events, which led us to the beginning of the fifth century. In fact, throughout the fourth century, there was tension between the new religion of the state and certain parts of the country that were still tied to pagan religions. Some catholicoi were even martyred by pagans. In that process, Saint Nersess the Great played an important role. In 353, he organized a council that effected many reforms, created charitable institutions (hospitals, orphanages, etc.) and created rules for monasteries.

So that process of conversion saw its apogee in the beginning of the fifth century with Saint Mesrob's invention of the alphabet and the great translations of the Scriptures and liturgical texts. It was at that moment that the people saw their religion in this new faith. That was the accomplishment of the enculturation. Before then, the people were not familiar with the new religion, since the literature was celebrated in Greek or in Syriac and there was not a translation of the Bible yet. The Christian faith, expressed and communicated in Armenian, penetrated the hearts and lives of the people, who were able to hear the Word of God in their language. As Koriun, the biographer of Saint Mesrob Mashtots, says: "God spoke Armenian."

Noah and his ark

So your Church goes back, if not to the first century, which is very likely, then at least to the beginning of Christianity. However, Armenia's spiritual history intersected with the story of salvation well before that.

In his book Il Milione, which describes "the wonders of the world," my fellow countryman Marco Polo, who visited your country between 1271 and 1276 on his way to China, tells us that "in Greater Armenia is Noah's Ark, on a large mountain on the southern border." Many names of ancient Armenian cities are linked to the story of the flood, Noah and the ark. Beyond what is legend, history, tradition, what is the meaning of this link between the Armenian Church and the Old Testament?

Mount Ararat is mentioned more than once in the Old Testament, but by that name, one did not only mean the mountain, but also the territory around it, the kingdom of Ararat, which historians identify with Urartu, the denomination of our land before the arrival of the Armens in the seventh century B.C.

The tradition of Noah has occupied a central place in the spirituality of the Armenian people. Our ancient chroniclers present the origin of the people as deriving from Noah's lineage. That explains our attachment to that tradition, which makes our land a biblical one. For our people, Mount Ararat and Noah's Ark have become a symbol of eternity, a sign of God's presence here in the person of Noah. If Mount Ararat has inspired so many of our poets and artists, it is because we identify it with tenacity, perseverance and also with our people's desire for eternity.

The irony today, of course, is that Mount Ararat is no longer in Armenia...

Only from the geographical perspective!

The question of Monophysitism

Allow me to return to Marco Polo. He writes about Armenians: "They are Christian: Jacobites and Nestorians." It seems to me that those are two different, opposing doctrines.

Marco Polo was a great traveler, historian, and even an ethnographer... but a mediocre theologian! Maybe he confused the Armenians with other people who lived close to us. Whatever the case may be, the Armenian Church has never been Nestorian, nor Monophysite in the sense used by Eutyches. Today, that is universally recognized.

In its Christology, our Church has adopted the line of Alexandrian theology. In the beginning, there were two theological currents at the heart of the Armenian Church: Antiochian and Alexandrian. In the end, Alexandrian theology overtook the other. We Armenians were not able to participate in the Christological quarrels of the fourth and fifth centuries. In the fourth century, our Church was still being formed. In the fifth century, we were involved in the resistance against Mazdeism, which was threatening to return. The participation of our Church in the Council of Nicaea is proved by the fact that our representative Aristakes, the son of Saint Gregory, was one of the signers of the Nicene Creed; but we did not participate in the two other ecumenical Councils of Constantinople and Ephesus, nor in the Council of Chalcedon.

However, we were not ignorant of what was happening, since we had Armenians who were studying theology in Constantinople and in other centers of the Christian East. But our Church's position on Christology was not formulated until the beginning of the sixth century, in 506, which I tried to show in my book *The Council of Chalcedon and the Armenian Church*. From the fourth century until the end of the fifth, the development of theology in Armenia was moving in a direction that excluded the acceptance of the duality of natures, formulated in 451 at the Council of Chalcedon, and particularly in the *Tome* of Pope Leo I. The Armenians saw in these formulations a new wave of Nestorianism. Later, the Neo-Chalcedonian movement sought to interpret the formulations of the Council of Chalcedon as not being opposed to the teachings of Saint Cyril of Alexandria.

The Armenian Church is not Monophysite in the usual sense of the word: that is to say, in the sense of recognizing a single divine nature of Christ with a virtual annihilation of His humanity — which, according to Eutyches, would be lost in His divinity "like a drop of honey in the ocean." We do not follow Nestorius either, since we have never accepted duality in the person of Christ, the Word Incarnate, which Nestorius did not know how to get past. The proof of that is that in our liturgical texts, we anathematize Eutyches, Nestorius and their doctrines. As for Christology, we remain in the current of Saint Cyril of Alexandria's theology.

You say that you are not Monophysite in Eutyches' sense; at the same time, you do not accept the Council of Chalcedon, which condemned it. Are you Monophysite in another sense, different from Eutyches' doctrine?

It all depends on the meaning you give that word. If one understands Monophysitism as professing "one nature of God, the Word incarnate," as a union of two natures, then in that case, we are Monophysite. But that word has acquired a "Eutychian" connotation; it is so charged with its historical use as an expression of Eutyches' doctrine, which we rejected, that we don't like to be called Monophysite.

So you are saying that at the very moment of the Incarnation, divine nature and human nature are united inseparably in the Son incarnate in a single nature.

Yes, but "in a single nature" means in a single person. The two natures haven't lost their own characteristics or their integrity, but they do not act separately; otherwise, we would have a dualism, and the Incarnation would not have taken place.

It seems to me that this concerns a question of terminology: the unified nature (Monophysitism) that you claim to be the union of two natures, which corresponds to what the Chalcedonian churches define as a single person in whom the two natures are united.

That is very evident.

A long misunderstanding

Nevertheless, you were considered Monophysite in the heretical sense by the rest of Christianity from the year 451. Is this a question of a misunderstanding? A misunderstanding of 1,550 years?

In the time of the conflict surrounding the formulations of Chalcedon, theologians and others responsible for the churches involved were very sincere in their teachings. But with the development of theological thought, when we were able to establish a true dialogue, consisting of a reciprocal openness, the other churches stated several times that our "Monophysitism" was *not* heretical, as they had suspected. For example, in the twelfth century there was a very close theological relationship between the Church of Constantinople and the center of our Church, which was in Hromgla at the time, between Armenia and Cilicia. That exchange, promoted by our Catholicos Saint Nersess the Gracious, one of the most lucid and faithful theologians of our Church, must be understood today as a model of ecumenical dialogue.

In the exhibition of the Armenian doctrine that Saint Nersess presented to Emperor Manuel I Comnenus, there is a key expression:

> If one says "a nature" in the sense of an indissoluble and indivisible nature, and not in the sense of confusion, and if one says "two natures" as being without confusion and without alteration and not meaning "division," then both positions are within the sphere of orthodoxy.

So I think that on the theological level, the misunderstanding was cleared up at that time. On the other hand, you know very well that the impressions, the reminiscences and suspicions of the past have a long life, and it is very difficult to forget them. In the nineteenth century, people wrote a lot on that subject. The great Lutheran theologian of the turn of the century, Adolf von Harnack, showed that the Armenians are not Monophysite in Eutyches' sense. In the non-religious press, people have continued to say that the Armenian Church is Monophysite. All the same, I think that today, for well informed theologians, the misunderstanding has dissipated and disappeared.

Why, in 451, did you not accept the Council of Chalcedon?

First of all, Armenians were not invited to give an opinion on the subject. I have already said that we were involved in the defense of our Christian faith against Mazdeism, and 451 was the date of the Battle of Avarayr against the Persians. Even though that battle was decisive for the history of Armenia, the threat posed by the Persians continued until the end of the century. The Armenians pursued a guerilla resistance and it was not until 484 that we were truly autonomous from the Mazdean hegemony.

But at that time, there was the Edict of Zeno, the *Henoticon* (AD 482), which meant a distancing from the strict line of the Council. You must not forget that several theological schools, like the Church of Alexandria, vigorously contested Chalcedon. It was not a universally accepted Council, which is why we did not necessarily have to make the decision to accept or reject it. When we saw that Nestorianism was gaining ground because of the Council of Chalcedon, we rejected that Council, which in 506 was presented in a way that justified the theology of Nestorius without using his name.

So one of the reasons why you did not accept Chalcedon and the following Councils was the fact that the Christian world was not entirely represented there.

Yes. Chalcedon and the Councils that followed were seen by the Armenian, Coptic, Syrian and Ethiopian churches as particular Councils, in the sense that they were dealing with the lives and responsibilities of the participating churches, and thus could not be seen as universal.

Similarly, after the seventh Council recognized by the Byzantine churches, the Roman Church had several others that they call *ecumenical*, but they are considered by the Orthodox churches as particular Councils, having to do with the Church of Rome.

So you have not exactly rejected the decisions of those Councils?

We simply have not taken a position on their subjects, since for us they are the particular Councils of the churches that convened them. Surely in the ecumenical dialogue of today, we should consider the teaching of these Councils to explore the questions they raise.

The declaration in Rome

Let's return to our era. In the month of December 1996, something happened that some people have qualified as a historical event. You, as the Catholicos of All Armenians, with a great number of bishops of your Church, went to Rome on a brotherly visit to the head of the Roman Catholic Church, and you signed a "Common Declaration." What was it about? What is the significance of that declaration?

First of all, that visit was one of many made between heads of churches. My predecessor, Catholicos Vasken, had visited Pope Paul VI in the same manner. These visits were made in the context of ecumenical relations and in the hope of strengthening the bond between our churches.

With Pope John Paul II we made a declaration in which we repeated what our fathers had already said before us. We expressed our common Christology together, by affirming that Jesus Christ is perfect God and perfect man, and that His divinity is one with His humanity in a real and perfect union.

Your declaration says that you were making note of the great progress made by both churches "in the common pursuit of unity in Christ, the Word of God in flesh. Perfect God in His divinity, perfect man in His humanity, His divinity is one with His humanity in the person of the only Son of God in a real, perfect union without confusion, without alteration, without division, without a single form of separation." These last words are direct quotes from the Chalcedonian formula. Haven't you changed your mind?

No. Those words were used by our fathers in many theological treatises, since we have always said that there was no confusion in the natures of the person of the Word Incarnate. It is true that these words are also in the formulation of Chalcedon, but they express what the Church believed before the Council. On the other hand, there were other aspects of Chalcedon that were adopted as norms of the faith, but that we do not accept; particularly in Pope Leo's *Letter to Flavian* [i.e. the *Tome* of Leo], where he describes the two natures as each having their own operations. But the formulation that you have quoted also appears in the dogmatic formulations of the fathers of all Eastern churches. So what we said with Pope John Paul II is not really anything new; our theologians have recognized that we have different formulations, but the same Christology.

How was the Common Declaration received by the members of your Church?

In general, the reception was positive. There were criticisms, but they were not well founded. For example, the most significant criticism was that we should not have said that the two natures were unified "in the person of the only Son," but rather "in the person of Christ." Christ being the only Son of God, that critique does not make much sense. That type of critique does not have any real weight.

Here, I would like to play the role of the man on the street. I understand that in the first centuries of Christianity, it was very important to express and to defend the content of our faith in the Trinity, in Jesus Christ, etc. But you have to say to yourself that in our times, for the vast majority of our contemporaries, including the believers of all churches, these disputes do not seem to be very useful. The man in the street often has the impression that the churches lose themselves in insignificant debates instead of rolling up their sleeves and spreading the message of Christ to society.

I see that situation very clearly, and I must admit that I sympathize with those people who cannot understand the meaning of these theological nuances, of the subtleties of these formulations. Today what counts is faith that is alive and not one form or another. The people are waiting for us, the leaders of churches, to be united in the service of the same Lord.

But that is exactly why theological studies are necessary, to clear the path for unity. As for Christology, we believe that in spite of the differences in our formulations, we have the same faith in the same person of Christ, as the only Son of God incarnate who assumed our humanity. Now, it's the strength of our preaching of that faith in Christ that is important. But there are other differences between the two churches outside of Christology. The fundamental issue in our relationship with the Church of Rome is that of the authority in the Church and of other dogmatic formulations of the Catholic Church. Together, we must study these differences in order to arrive at unity.

What is the status of your relationships with other Eastern churches? How do orthodox Chalcedonians see the Armenian Church?

Concerning the question of Christology, the two families of orthodox churches—that is, the Chalcedonian churches from the Byzantine tradition and the non-Chalcedonian churches—have held official and semi-official theological consultations, and there has been great progress toward a mutual understanding. Today, the conclusions of those theological consultations must be studied officially by the heads of the orthodox churches.

Apart from the Christological aspect, which seems to have been cleared up, there are other, historical issues that we must resolve. For example, if one of the conditions for the establishment of unity of our churches is the acceptance of all the Councils following the third, then that poses a great problem to us. I would say that, generally, our churches are on the path to a mutual understanding. The liturgical differences between our traditions are not an obstacle to unity.

How many Armenian churches?

I would like to talk now about your ecclesiastical structure. You have four sees, with two Patriarchates and two Catholicossates. What are the historical reasons that determined such an organization of the Church? Is there a single or several Armenian churches?

There is only one Armenian Church, which has the Catholicossate of All Armenians as its spiritual center. This

Catholicossate, the premier and original, was the only one until the fifteenth century. Before that time, there were other Catholicossates, due to the historical circumstances of our national life, but they had a local jurisdiction. That was the case, for example, for the Catholicossate of Aghtamar (an island in lake Van in Eastern Armenia, today in Turkey), which existed in the twelfth and thirteenth centuries, whose jurisdiction was limited to the region of Van, Vaspouragan. Similarly, there were other Catholicossates that lasted for a few years or decades and that disappeared when the circumstances making them necessary changed.

An important event took place in the fifteenth century. The Catholicossate of All Armenians was located, from the eleventh century, outside of Armenia Major, in a territory known as Cilicia. In 1293, the See of All Armenians moved to Sis, the capital of the kingdom of Cilicia. In 1375, with the capture of Sis, the Kingdom of Cilicia was destroyed by the Mamelukes; the Catholicossate remained in Sis, but they were already thinking of transferring it to Holy Etchmiadzin. At that time, the Church of Rome, through the Crusaders and the religious orders, had tried to spread propaganda that the Armenians of Armenia disapproved of strongly. This pushed our Church to transfer its center to Etchmiadzin in 1441. The Catholicos of Sis, Gregory IX, being advanced in age, did not want to move there personally. So a national ecclesiastical assembly elected a new Catholicos of All Armenians in Etchmiadzin. A few years after the death of Gregory IX, a new Catholicos was chosen in Cilicia for that region that did not depend politically on Armenia. The Catholicossate continued to exist, but its jurisdiction was limited to the former Cilicia.

In 1920, when the Armenians abandoned Cilicia and sought refuge in Syria and Lebanon, the Catholicos left Sis, and for nine years did not have a fixed seat. Finally, he established himself in Antelias, close to Beirut, and with the consent of the Catholicos of All Armenians, received a certain number of churches in Lebanon and Syria from the Armenian Patriarchate of Jerusalem. Thus, three countries found themselves under his jurisdiction: Syria, Lebanon and Cyprus.

And the two other Patriarchates?

The Patriarchate of Jerusalem has existed for a long time: as a local church since the fourth or fifth centuries, but as a patriarchate it was recognized in the fourteenth century. That Patriarchate had charge of the safety of the holy places, and of the spiritual care of pilgrims who went to the Holy City. In addition, today its jurisdiction also includes the Armenian community of Jordan.

The Patriarchate of Constantinople, which has been established by order of the conqueror of Constantinople, the Sultan Fatih Muhammed in 1461, became, after the fall of the Ottoman Empire and the proclamation of the state of Atatürk, the spiritual center for the Armenians of Turkey.

To summarize: your ecclesiastical system is due to historical circumstances; the Armenian Church is a single church with its spiritual center at Holy Etchmiadzin, and the other sees today are founded on a repartitioning of territories and keep their title of Patriarchcate and (in the case of the See of Cilicia) of Catholi-cossate for reasons of historical fidelity.

However, it seems to me that in some cases, the territories of the two Catholicossates would coincide, for example in America.

Again, you must go back to the historical circumstances. In 1930, the See of Cilicia was reestablished in Antelias, in Lebanon, as a local Catholicossate, independent in the affairs concerning its jurisdiction. In 1956, there were attempts by the Soviet state to control the See of Cilicia and to exploit it for ideological propaganda; to that end, the Communists used the name and prestige of the Mother See of Etchmiadzin. The Catholicossate of Cilicia opposed those attempts, and, as a young priest, I defended the administrative independence of that see, where I had had my sacerdotal education and where I served as a priest, bishop and even as a catholicos. Faced with this conflict, some communities of the diaspora, not wanting to stay under the jurisdiction of an ecclesiastical see that was being used by the Soviets to promote political objectives, asked the Catholicossate of Cilicia to be taken under its jurisdiction. That was the case for Iran and Greece.

It was a little different for America. During the Cold War between the two great powers, and in particular after the odious assassination of the Armenian archbishop of New York in 1933, a part of the Armenian community of America formed an autonomous prelacy that was not recognized by any of the patriarchal sees. But in 1957, when the conflict between the two Catholicossates began, those American communities joined the See of Cilicia.

These are the political reasons that I just mentioned that explain the situation of our Church in these countries;

among the communities that belong to different jurisdic-
tions, there is not a single dogmatic, liturgical, or canonical
difference.

The jurisdictional quarrels have served their time...

*Nevertheless, the fact that there are two parallel hierarchies of the
same church might disorient your followers... Do you envision a
different way of organizing the Church in these countries?*

Discussions are underway among the dioceses in question.
There is an inter-diocesan committee that is working on a
solution to that problem.   Now, without the political
reasons that we had before, I hope that we will be able to
achieve unity on the structural level, by reforming the two
parallel structures as a single diocese under the jurisdiction of the Catholicossate of All Armenians.

*What was your relationship with Vasken I, the Catholicos of All
Armenians when you were the Catholicos of Cilicia?*

In 1977, the Catholicossate of All Armenians participated
in my election as Catholicos of Cilicia with two votes, as
provided by the Constitution of the See of Cilicia and the
practice of old times; similarly, the Catholicossate of Cilicia
has always had two votes in the election of the Catholicos
of All Armenians. This is a symbolic way of expressing the
unity of the Church.

   After my election, I wrote a letter to Catholicos Vasken,
in which I expressed my fraternal love and my availability

to work together. Later, I met with him personally in Paris in 1984. It was an unofficial two-day meeting, very open and brotherly, during which we discussed certain jurisdictional problems existing between our Catholicossates. It was 1984, and the Catholicossate of Etchmiadzin was still under the Soviet regime; at that time, the only thing that we could do was maintain a fraternal relationship. Then, during the summer of 1988, we met a second time in Moscow during the celebration of the millennium of the baptism of Russia, with the two Armenian Patriarchs from Jerusalem and Constantinople. At that time, the Karabagh movement had already begun; the Catholicos invited us to come to Armenia to show the solidarity of the Church in the diaspora with the Armenian people. I accepted, but since the two Patriarchs had trouble getting there right away, we postponed the visit to a later date. Then, in October of 1988, the Catholicos wrote me a letter with an official invitation to Etchmiadzin for the beginning of 1989. Shortly after our meeting in Moscow, we named two delegations (from Etchmiadzin and Antelias), which met and studied the divergences between the two sees in a fraternal spirit.

After that, events evolved in an unforeseen manner because of the earthquake of December 1988. From the beginning, there was a large mobilization on the part of the diaspora: I visited Holy Etchmiadzin personally, and I sent a letter to the dioceses within the jurisdiction of the See of Cilicia asking everyone to direct their help to the Catholicossate of Etchmiadzin. Many of our bishops of Cilicia went to Armenia to show their solidarity with the Catholicos of All Armenians. That created an environment conducive to the solution of our problems.

My personal relations with Catholicos Vasken were always very amicable. I remember as if it were yesterday when, in 1956, he came to Antelias for the election of the Catholicos of Cilicia. I was still a young priest. On February 14, the day of the celebration of the Presentation of Jesus at the temple, I celebrated the liturgy, and at the end, in accordance with our rite, I brought him holy bread. He asked me my name and congratulated me for bearing the name Karekin in honor of Catholicos Karekin Hovsepian. Later he told me that, from that first meeting, he always felt sympathetic toward me. Myself, I always had great respect for the patience and perseverance with which he guided the Church in spite of all the pressures of the Communist state. That mutual sympathy helped us to build unity between us.

Having once been the Catholicos of Cilicia, you have become the Catholicos of All Armenians. Does your relationship to your successor in Cilicia continue in the same manner? Are you working toward a deeper unity between the two Catholicossates?

First I must say that I know the new Catholicos, Aram I, very well, since he was one of my students at the Seminary of Antelias and then my assistant as the archbishop of Lebanon. I have always appreciated him for his devotion to the Church, to theology and ecumenism. Our relations today continue in an atmosphere of esteem, fraternity and intimacy. At the time of his election in July 1995, I went to Antelias and I presided over the ceremony of his consecration. After his election, he visited me twice here at the Holy See of Etchmiadzin; also, we met each other in Paris.

Recently, a delegation from Antelias came to Holy Etchmiadzin at our invitation and had some discussions with the delegation from our Holy See. So the discussions continue, and I hope that they will soon prove fruitful, since our people need this unity, and the jurisdictional questions, after the creation of a free and independent Armenia, have served their time.

The new generation

After the genocide of 1915 and the exodus from Cilicia in 1920, many Armenians found refuge in the United States, in Europe, and in other countries of the world. Since they are much more spread out than in the Near East, the descendants of those refugees have begun to forget their language. Today, the fourth generation of those Armenians in many cases knows neither the language nor the culture of their fathers and, consequently, has very weak links to your Church.

Do you believe that those young people will completely forget their origins?

Being myself a child of the diaspora, I understand the situation of the young people you are talking about very well. Those Armenians are much more integrated in the lives of the countries they live in — whether in Europe or in North or South America, in the Near East or in Australia and New Zealand — than our generation was. Some have been able to keep Armenian as a second language, thanks to the courses organized by Armenian communities. However, there are cases in which our youth do not speak Armenian at all any more.

But language is not the only link with the historic motherland: there is Armenian culture, our folklore, dance, and especially our Armenian family traditions. I personally have met many Armenians in the United States who no longer spoke the language but who kept many of the traditions of family life, holidays, etc. For those people, the Church is the principal home of their Armenian culture. And that is natural. The Church is the guarantor of Armenianness, in the sense of belonging to our nation; everyone can find the Christian faith expressed in our own cultural traditions there, a faith that is still alive, since we are not a Church of the past.

So you believe that, through the means of the Church, new generations of Armenians of the diaspora can keep that relationship with their origins.

Yes. The feeling of Armenianness is not completely lost in the diaspora. In human psychology, the desire to go back to one's origins is something innate.

But the question of the new generation of the diaspora that you asked is of great significance to me: how can the young people of the diaspora situate their Armenian roots in the cultural context of the society in which they were born or raised?

Today, thanks to the development of communications, different cultures intertwine much more than they did in the past. From that perspective, the creation of an independent Armenia, open to the diaspora, is something of great importance. The dream of several centuries has been realized; our youth now has a home, that of their ancestors, which is a free, open country that is not locked up behind an Iron Curtain. Thus many young Armenians from abroad come to visit the country of their fathers. For the two and a half years that I have been Catholicos here, the happiest times for me were my meetings with groups of young people to whom I have repeated that our country and our Church are a home for them, even for those who do not speak our language.... They feel at home when they are in the heart of their Mother Church, as one young person from Canada told me.

I think that in recent years, the bond between the diaspora and the mother country has become much more intense.

Post-Soviet syndrome

Let's return to the diaspora in Armenia. I would like to talk about the situation of your country after Communism. In many of the republics of the ex-Soviet Union, there is a problem concerning the moral order. Communism, not truly having surrendered, was not subjected to a moral evaluation, a historical judgment. In Russia, the communists disguised themselves as democrats, the bureaucrats disguised themselves as businessmen, the atheists as passionate Orthodox... In that type of "masquerade," the Church finds itself at a crossroads of all kinds of political forces which wish to invite it to dance. The greatest danger today comes from political opposition – that is, communists who continue to call themselves such and nationalists. They seek to exploit the Church, to use it as a national emblem...

What is the relationship of your Church with the State and with the political forces in post-Soviet Armenia?

You are posing a very delicate question. I am not very familiar with the situation of the Russian Church after Communism, nor the relationship of Church and State in Russia; I was not very familiar with the situation of the Russian Church before the change, either. As for Armenia today, the new generation of leaders who have assumed the responsibilities of the state is composed for the most part of people who, before the end of the Soviet era, had revolted against the regime. Among them are intellectuals who know the history and culture of our people very well and who know that Armenianness is inseparable from Christian values. Unfortunately, these people do not have the opportunity to really get to know the Church, to experience in person this communal life filled with faith that is the true essence of the Church.

In Armenia, Communism was never an ideology espoused by Armenians. It was imposed. Communism was always seen here as a foreign ideology that we were obligated to accept. Atheist propaganda in Armenia was very strong, as it was everywhere in the Soviet Union; it eliminated the teaching of faith as well as any public religious expression. However, it was not able to extinguish the Christian conscience of the people.

I was here three times during the Communist regime and I saw in person the way that faith persisted in people's hearts. I saw mothers giving an arm and a leg to have their children blessed by a bishop. I even saw an attic converted into a church, with a book of prayers hidden under some straw, and when the peasants were alone, they would take out the book and pray together. When they were preaching atheism on television, people turned it off. Overall, in spite of the propaganda of the state, people were attached to their faith. All of Armenian culture bears witness to the Christian faith: our ancient manuscripts, our architecture, our music, our crosses carved in stone, our famous *khatchkars*. Even a closed church speaks of God...

As for the relationship between Church and State, the current leaders of our country, having experienced the Soviet state which sought to manipulate the Church, will not repeat that error, since the confusion between Church and State does not serve the interest of either group. The Armenian State is organized as a secular one. Nevertheless, the cooperation of the Church and State is necessary, and the Church must be integrated into national life.

The problem with extreme nationalism seems to exist in many Orthodox countries. Recently, the French Orthodox theologian Olivier Clément analyzed this problem:

> *Nationalism exasperated by centuries of more or less multinational empires has wanted to appropriate Orthodoxy, make it its tool, instill in it its hatred, its fears, its fantasies. Often, Orthodoxy has become the cement of one's affiliation to their country, a little like Judaism in the State of Israel. They like the forests of their native land, the chants of the churches and the flames of the candles, but they have never read the Gospel. They call themselves Orthodox (while specifying their nationality) but we hardly know that they are Christian. They might even call themselves Orthodox and be atheists!*

One of the most frequent images in the demonstrations in the streets of Moscow is that of the red flags and the portraits of Stalin next to the icons...

Olivier Clément's statement seems to me to generalize particular situations. In Armenian history, the Church was never a slave to the state as might have been the case in Russia in the time of Peter the Great and the emperors who succeeded him. In Armenia, we have never had a strong central power, like a czar or an emperor, who could exploit the Church. Throughout the difficult history of our people, the Church was identified with the fate of the nation.

The allusion that Olivier Clément makes here concerning this combination of faith, the Gospel and a sense of national affiliation is very important. Of course, you cannot say that you are Orthodox *and* atheist. To reduce Orthodoxy to a national emblem or to the manifestation of a people's culture, to the same level as folklore, is not to have met God. Belonging to Orthodoxy, before being one's affiliation to this or that Church or orthodox nation, is belonging to Christ. But the issue of the interrelation between faith and national identity is much more complex and subtle than people think. In our case, with the teaching of Christ having penetrated the historical experience of our people so existentially, the sense of national affiliation is not really separable from faith and the Church. That is often the case for our Eastern churches, which — we must not forget — are national churches. But it is natural that in coming out of a regime that spoke and acted in the name of an artificial internationalism, and that sought to erase all unity from the peoples it subjugated, nationalism can sometimes degenerate into intolerance and exclusivism. But in terms of a sense of belonging to a culture and to a people, nationalism is not a negative phenomenon.

What is happening now in Armenia, as in other countries of the ex-Soviet Union, is that some people, because of the communist past, see the Christian faith as an ideology. Thus, the churches must, through preaching, help these people to correct that opinion. You know very well that the Christian faith is, I would say, *incarnational*, through the very person of our Lord, who was the Word Incarnate. Christian preaching, in countries that come from the Soviet regime, must in my opinion be oriented above all toward the aspects of faith that are directly related to real life, that touch people and society today.

That is how I think the Armenian Church can and must contribute to the recovery of the nation and the state, through the moral principles that will build a solid foundation for the nation.

We will return later to the question of nationalism. For now, I would like to continue with the problems of a post-Soviet society. In your opinion, what are the most obvious traces left behind by the seventy years of that regime?

I think that the first consequence of the Communist collectivism was the loss of the value of man's dignity, of the human being. With its ambitious objective of constructing a new world based on Marxist ideology, Communism ignored the value of the human being as an individual, seeing only the interest of the whole, the State. But human dignity—of man *as an individual*—is something that we cannot ignore or denigrate. We must give back to everyone a sense of dignity. The reorganization of public life must be geared towards reestablishing that value, beginning with education.

The same goes for an individual's confidence in himself, in his ability to work, to be responsible for his own life, to dedicate himself to personal initiatives. We must get back the feeling that our destiny is in our hands. The State in socialist countries was an entity that oppressed the people, and consequently the people had an attitude of silent, hidden opposition. On the other hand, since everything was controlled by the State, they hoped for and expected everything from the State. That still continues today. Often I ask people who complain that the State doesn't do this or that: *who is the State?* The State is what we want it to be; the State is what we have made it through our own involvement.

In the countries of the diaspora, we have had the experience of a change of attitude. We have gone beyond the mentality of being second-class citizens, refugees, exiles, and have arrived at a mature social awareness, as citizens enjoying full rights, engaged in public life. I think that an evolution must take place now in Armenia. This country of thirty thousand square kilometers is entrusted to us, and we are responsible for it. If something doesn't work, we cannot shrug our shoulders and say, "That's Moscow's responsibility," or place the responsibility on Turkey, as our ancestors did during the Ottoman empire... Today we can only blame ourselves! But it would be better to roll up our sleeves and get into the thick of things, not only in material rebuilding, but also in this change of perspective, in a new understanding of our national spirit.

Overall, I think that today our nation needs a *metanoia,* an interior conversion.

Do you believe that that will require a long process – longer than a generation?

It will certainly take some time. But the speed of that evolution also depends on the intensity of our efforts; we cannot leave everything to time. We must always aim towards being more responsible for ourselves, to go beyond that mentality of dependence.

Liberty without responsibility cannot be true and complete; we must find the elements in our national psychology that can help us assume our responsibilities. In the past, our people maintained their Armenianness under much more difficult circumstances; we must emphasize and rediscover that tenacity, that perseverance in our commitment and our work. One of the most important goals must be to find the means by which everyone can earn a living through their work, since that would mean that they can rediscover their own dignity.

The Catholicos and renewal

In that process, it seems to me that the very existence of the Armenian diaspora proves to be providential. It is like a reservoir of human power that can help Armenia. I am not alluding to the possibility of material help, but to the fact that the millions of Armenians spread out all over the world have had a different life experience that they can share with their Armenian brothers, a different education, a different mindset.

Allow me to add frankly that it is possible that having a Catholicos in the See of Holy Etchmiadzin who is an Armenian of the diaspora also works in this manner...

The diaspora is a great force today for our country. I am very happy to see that since the proclamation of independence, our brothers and sisters of the diaspora have done a lot for Armenia. You are very right to say that their participation has not only been in terms of a material contribution, but above all, a human sharing. The Armenians of the diaspora can share with us their wealth of competence —in the domains of work, technology, intellectual and cultural life—that they have acquired thanks to their experience in the different countries of the world. The wall separating Armenia from the diaspora has been demolished; but there is still a lot to do. It is the time to build bridges, create contacts; the key to our renewal lies in the solidarity of our nation.

Holiness, what is the meaning of your election? As Christians, we believe that the election expresses the will of God, and the Assembly that elected you heard the voice of the Holy Spirit. Nevertheless, there are surely some human motivations involved in the choice. In choosing a person who has always lived in another country, did the Armenian Church want to free itself from the weight of the previous seventy years? Or rather, did it want to open itself up to the West, to other churches, to accept the challenge of renewal? Or again, is it simply the victory of the diaspora over post-Soviet Armenia? Or the will of God to reconcile the two Catholicossates in conflict?

It seems to me that it would be necessary to ask the people who voted... For the most part, the voters were Armenians from Armenia and from countries of the former Soviet Union. I suppose that all of the causes that you mentioned played a role in my election. But for me, their choice has a single meaning: the duty to offer everything that God and my forty-five years of ministry in the Church have given me to the service of the people.

I think that many of the people who participated in the election thought that the experience I had acquired as a priest, bishop and Catholicos of Cilicia could be useful and add a certain momentum to the process of renewal in our Church and our country. The confidence that they demonstrated in me has obligated me, before all else, to always be humble. By accepting the will of the people, which expresses the will of God, I asked the Lord to give me everything I would need to respond to the expectations of my people. From the beginning, I knew that it would be a difficult task, but in these two and a half years, I can say that it has been much more difficult than I thought...

What is your assessment of the two and a half years of your Catholicossate? What are your objectives for the future?

Today in Armenia, what is in question is the veritable image of the Church. The Church is not something from the past, which is what they wanted people to believe for seventy years. Nor is it a static institution, but an active presence in the lives of our people.

Our top priority right now is to reinvigorate the service of the Church by encouraging the formation of a new generation of dedicated priests and lay people. That is why I have begun to reorganize the seminary. By the grace of God, many young people have responded to His call. But there is still much to do, particularly to improve the quality of education. The seminary is the priority in my concerns.

Next to that, the second thing has been the creation of a Center of Christian Education for lay people, which must produce teachers of religion for schools. The Gospel is not a treasure of the past, a beautiful illuminated manuscript; it is the message of God, which must be lived in our individual, familial, communal, and national lives. That is why the Church's preaching must not be the proclamation of a theory or ideological propaganda. For me, the word *preaching* is synonymous with engagement, service, action. That means that the methodology we use to announce God's message must be changed.

A third concern involves the cultural service in which the Church must engage itself, since in Armenia you cannot separate culture and religion. We have given a great importance to publishing and to the publications of the Catholicossate. That is something that I undertook in Antelias as well, when I was the Catholicos of Cilicia. Now, we publish mostly the writings of our Fathers translated into modern Armenian, as well as didactic texts: sermons, meditations, explanations of the liturgy, etc.

We have done a lot, and there is still much to do in the work of rebuilding parishes, renovating old churches and building new ones. That is important because it will give a meeting place to each community: Christian faith is above all a community life. That is why we must rediscover the very notion of the parish, which was completely eradicated in the Soviet era. Similarly, it is necessary to reorganize the lives of the dioceses and to establish new ones, in Armenia as well as the diaspora.

Finally, there is the social aspect, or, as we say in the Church, the diaconate. People talk a lot about *koinonia*, about *kerygma*, but the diaconate must be the outcome of our relationship with God and the announcement of Christ. It is through service that the *koinonia* and the *kerygma* are expressed concretely. Our Church is still weak in this area because of our lack of material means. The service to the poor, to the handicapped, the ill, the elderly, the needy, is part of the solicitude for man that Christ demonstrated and that the Church must pursue. Under Communism, our Church did no work in the social realm, since it was forbidden. So we must start at the beginning. Unfortunately, the economic situation is a determining factor; we do not have any permanent means, and everything that the Church had in the past was confiscated by the Communist state. However, we have already begun, thanks especially to the help of the Armenians of the diaspora and of ecumenical groups. We are grateful to all those who help us and are convinced that God will also help us accomplish this task.

Facing the future

People often say that Armenians know their history perfectly and that for each monument, church or khatchkar *(a cross of stone), they know the date, the artist, etc. During my stay in Etchmiadzin, I had the opportunity to see that that is indeed true. However, while speaking here with your seminarians and young deacons, I saw that although they know the history of Armenia*

very well, they are not limited by the nostalgia of a glorious past,
but on the contrary, they are very open to ecumenical dialogue
and to the challenges of modern society. Overall, my impression
as an outside observer is that while the Armenian Church looks
at its past of saints and martyrs with pride, it would like to see
the future with the same pride.

I am delighted by what you are saying since it encourages
me to stay on the path that we have chosen. I give thanks
to God when I see that among the youth, there is an awareness of our place in the world. In the past, people were not
familiar with the world like they are today. In our times,
the horizon of every person has become more vast, and all
those who are involved in the Church, thanks to our
contacts in the diaspora, as well as with ecumenical
groups, understand more and more that our Church must
be more active than it was in the past.

   People often speak of the tragic past of our land, of our
wars, persecutions, genocide, the Armenian dispersion,
etc. Today, our young people often rebel against these
eternal discussions: why must Armenia be presented as a
country of terror, of massacres and suffering? Yes, our
history is not the story of a land of milk and honey—there
were thorns in abundance... But today, we want to rediscover our vitality, our energy, our dignity. In the past
people spoke in the diaspora of "starving Armenians" and
even, in certain French milieu, of "dirty Armenians," since
we arrived in the West as persecuted, humiliated refugees.
But today, the Armenians in the West have established
themselves as entrepreneurs in the most diverse domains;
we have some great Armenian names, from the diaspora
and from our country, who have made people take notice.

What is happening now is that it is the new generation that is very aware of its dignity, and it is more optimistic and more open to the present and to the future since it wants to prove that our people are not a nation that should inspire pity.

You election to the See of Etchmiadzin happened at a very particular and particularly happy moment in the history of your country. Seventy years of Communist dictatorship ended, Armenia won its independence, the Armenian Church seems to have reclaimed its unity after decades of misunderstandings and tensions, the other churches are beginning to accept it more completely, the ecumenical dialogue is firmly rooted. Also, the jubilee of two thousand years of Christianity is very close, and another jubilee awaits your Church: that of one thousand, seven hundred years of adhesion to the Christian faith, which you will celebrate in 2001.

All of these positive coincidences might explain the optimistic tone that people have perceived in your first public speeches. Beginning with the first, given upon your election at Etchmiadzin, and up through the sermon of your installation or your first encyclical. The optimism and the firm will of engagement, rolling up your sleeves – these seem to be the catch phrases of your speeches.

After two and a half years, are you still so optimistic?

Yes, I am an optimist; but at the same time a realist, I think, in the evaluation of the situation of our Church and our country. We still have enormous difficulties of every kind, but that is exactly why we must have that optimism, because you cannot resolve any problems with a resigned and defeatist attitude. History is not a source of consolation, but it must be a source of motivation and engagement. The economic conditions of our country are still at a level that leaves a lot to be desired; we must recognize and face this. But how do we approach such problems without optimism? If defeatism has a hold on us, then we are doomed from the start!

I believe that it is time for us to go beyond the temptation to complain and to have regrets, since that attitude cannot guide us in our task of reconstruction. However, the optimism that we need must not be Utopian, but an idealism that passes through realism. As I said in one of my first speeches, I always remember what Abraham Lincoln said: "The land that we have consecrated today is not for the dead, but for the living." We are now the masters of our country. We must commit ourselves passionately to the process of the recovery of our nation!

I am happy, and I thank God that I am the first Catholicos elected in a free country. But that carries an immense responsibility. This privilege is synonymous with duty, effort, and engagement.

CHAPTER V

The Word of God
& the Church

"The Gospel is our father…"

One of the maxims of the Armenian fathers says roughly the following: "The Gospel is our father, and the Church is our mother." Today I would like to talk about these two "parents."

What is the Gospel — and more generally, the Bible — in the Armenian tradition?

The maxim to which you are alluding belongs to Saint Vartan and the soldiers who died for the faith in the battle of Avarayr against the Persians in 451 and says, more precisely: "We recognize as our father the Holy Gospel and as our mother the Universal Apostolic Church." Thus, the Gospel is the father, he who gives general directives to his children, a sense of security and protection. The mother, the Church, nourishes the emotive constitution of her children through her tenderness and leaves an indelible mark on the formation of their moral character. Thus our national conscience, our culture and our spirituality were born and raised by these inseparable parents, the Gospel and the Church.

129

The Bible marked and guided the first steps of our literature. The very first lines that were written in the Armenian language, in the letters invented by Mesrob Mashtots, were the first verses of the Book of Proverbs: "To know wisdom and instruction, to perceive the words of intelligence...." As the famous Armenian historian and Byzantinist Nicholas Adonts noted,

> The Vulgate, for Latin countries, was not as important as the Armenian Bible for the Armenians. Latin literature had already existed for a long time before the Vulgate appeared. But the Armenian Bible ushered in a new era in the course of which the Armenians, learning how to use the pen, would take their place in civilization.

The formidable undertaking of the translation of the Word of God gave birth to our national literature and culture. Then the Fathers of the Church were translated, the liturgical texts, the hagiographic writings. Consequently, all of Armenian literature, including historiography, was marked in a unique manner by the spirit and the letter of the Bible.

The overwhelming majority of ancient Armenian manuscripts are of the Gospels; it is in this way that the words of Christ, translated into Armenian, have helped your people to protect their maternal language and their identity in spite of the invasions and the Turkish and Persian cultural pressures. Here is what the Russian Armenologist Kim Bakshi, who studied the numerous Armenian manuscripts in several libraries of the world, wrote about the role of the sacred literature in the formation of your national conscience:

> Constantly recopied, repeated thousands of times, always newly decorated, these innumerable gospels brought the values of Christianity to the people. For all of those who were humiliated, pillaged, forced to accept someone else's way of life and their foreign morals, these books spoke of the strength that each man has, of his liberty, of the force of his spirit. These books re-linked the Armenians to the great family of Christians, prevented them from falling out of the general movement of modern History that had begun with the Christ [...]. These thousands of manuscripts with a single content, and nothing else, saved the Armenian people and kept them within European civilization.

The manuscript of the sacred text thus played a religious and cultural role at the same time. But did the people of the Middle Ages have access to the Bible, since the manuscripts were the privilege of the elite?

These Gospels that, as Mr. Bakshi says, copied and decorated in an exemplary artistic manner, were naturally very expensive. The Scriptures were copied primarily for liturgical use; at church, one had to read the sacred texts. The hierarchs of the Church often wanted to have the Bible in their homes, for their personal use. Similarly, kings and queens, princes and princesses ordered the Bible from artists as a work of art as well as a book for reading. Also, in the monasteries, the formation of monks and students was based essentially on the Bible.

However, the knowledge of the Word of God, from the first centuries of our Christian history, was not limited to the more privileged classes of civilization, to the elite or the nobility. The Bible was also part of the everyday lives of the people, which is well established historically. Our writer from the fifth century Ghazar Parbetsi bears witness to the fact that people sang the Psalms in the streets. In the monastic schools, the Bible was the manual for everyday teaching. Long passages were learned by heart; in accordance with the rules set out by Saint Nersess the Gracious in his encyclical known as the *General Letter*, the priests had to recite all one hundred fifty psalms by heart. That explains the fact that our ecclesiastical authors from the classical times and from the Middle Ages quote the sacred text with stunning accuracy, without noting the chapters or verses.

The Bible has not only left an imprint on our cultural heritage, in the manuscripts and in the miniatures, but it also formed our conception of life. When I think about the role of the Bible in our Church and in the lives of the Armenian people, the image of the human body and the blood circulating within it comes to mind. As for liturgical life, aside from the fact that our liturgical calendar assigns three passages of the Scriptures to each day—from the Old Testament, the Gospels, and the Epistles—I must emphasize that many of our prayers reflect biblical texts. So that is how our Church has recognized the primordial status of the Bible in the lives of the people, in the national culture and in its liturgy.

I have developed that aspect of the status of the Bible in the lives and spirituality of the Armenian people in two chapters of my book, *In Search of Spiritual Life.*

The Sacred Book: talisman or source of inspiration?

You mentioned the liturgy. But what is the people's attitude toward the Bible, outside of the life of prayer?

Throughout history, the Bible enjoyed very great prestige among the rich and the aristocrats as well as among the less privileged strata of society. The colophon of a hand-written Armenian Bible tells us a story that eloquently describes the attitude of the people toward the Word of God: "Four brothers inherited a house from their father. This house could only be divided into three parts. But the father had also left a Bible. When the brothers drew lots to determine each person's part, the one who received the Bible was delighted by his good luck, and the other three envied him terribly..."

I would like to quote another example for you, taken from my family's life. We had the Bible in the house, and I remember that my mother read it frequently; that Bible belonged to my grandmother, who, being illiterate, could not read it. However, she kept the book, which had a mystical value... This tells us that for a long time, the approach of the faithful toward the Word of God was not limited to liturgical life; the Bible was in people's homes, and was present in family life.

A little story that you told in one of your sermons, I think in the United States, comes to mind. A child asks his mother, while pointing to a big, dusty book on the shelf: "Mama, is it true that that book is the book of God?" "Of course," replies the mother.

*"The Bible is the book of God." "Well then we should return it,"
says the child, "since we never read it."*

*You have emphasized that the people feel the sacred character
of the Bible. But do they read it? Is the Bible read today in
Armenia? I know that not too long ago, there was a translation
problem, the classical Armenian version being incomprehensible
to the people. What is the situation today?*

It is true that in the past the Bible did not reach as far is it
does today and that people did not read it as often in the
home. But we must not forget that in the Middle Ages,
people were, for the most part, illiterate and that before the
invention of printing by Gutenberg in the fifteenth century, the handwritten text was available only to the small
minority of the rich.

The first Bible printed in Armenian was in 1666; an
archbishop from Etchmiadzin went to live in Amsterdam
expressly to take care of this long job, which he achieved
with great success. Then there were other editions in 1733,
1805, and thanks also to the efforts of the Mekhitarist
Fathers, the Armenian Bible saw a wide distribution.
More recently, our Church, in association with the Bible
Society and similar organizations, has given new momentum to the distribution of the Bible.

Those editions were in the language that we call *grabar*,
classical Armenian, which the people do not understand so
well. The first translations into modern Armenian were
done by Protestant missionaries, but the quality of the
language was deplorable. Finally there were translations
done by our own Church, in Western Armenian and Eastern Armenian. In the last few decades, we have expanded
the production of biblical translations. Here at Holy

Etchmiadzin, modern Armenian translations of the New Testament as well as the whole text of the Bible, including the deuterocanonical books, have been reprinted several times. Thanks to the help of the Bible Society, we have been able to distribute over one hundred thousand New Testaments. The Catholicossate of Cilicia just completed a new translation of the New Testament in modern Western Armenian, and continues to work on the translation of the entire Bible.

So I would say that there is a tendency and a strong effort to make the Bible accessible to everyone. This involves the liturgy, as well. Even though liturgical language remains in classical Armenian, in many of our churches we perform the readings of the epistles of Saint Paul and of the other apostles in the modern language.

The Breath of God

In the Armenian tradition, the Scriptures are called the "Breath of God." According to what you just said, today the Scriptures are accessible to the followers of your Church and the Bible enjoys a good distribution.

So what people often say is no longer true: that Protestants read the Bible, the Orthodox read what liturgy quotes from the Bible, and Catholics read what Saint Augustine and Saint Thomas said about the Bible?

It is necessary first to reflect upon what we understand by "reading the Bible." Is it reading a book from which we individually draw our convictions? But that is normally what you do with any reading…. However, the Bible is not a book like other books, an ordinary reading. Let us not forget that the Bible is above all the living Word of God, the Breath of God, which was only committed to writing out of consideration for our human weakness.... The Bible is the living presence of God among us, and his text is a reminder. Thus the "intelligence of the Scriptures," from the Word of God, is not only the understanding, through our intellectual faculties, of the written text of the Bible. Here, real-life spiritual experience, the experience of every church, has a great significance. It is the Church that established the Canon, which distinguished the inspired books from others. In the same way, the Bible must be read in the context of the Church's life.

The liturgical calendar has always been centered around the Gospels; the Church proposes the passages concerning the birth of Christ for the Advent, the passages of the Passion and the Resurrection during the time of Lent and Easter. So the reading of the Bible, liturgical prayer and the lives of the people are all in harmony.

So the Armenian Church discourages its followers from reading the Bible individually?

Absolutely not. On the contrary, especially in recent times, with the new translations and editions of the Bible, our Church strongly advises people to read the Scriptures at home and outside of their liturgical use. We encourage the diffusion and distribution of the Bible by the most modern means; through our parishes, we have organized Bible study groups, open to everyone.

But at the same time, we insist on emphasizing that one must read the Bible not as a historical book, a philosophical book, or a literary work, but for what it truly is: the Word of God, which must be transformed into life.

"Believing is living": it is beautiful to remember that expression, so full of meaning! But the spiritual context of the Church, its thousand-year experience, helps us to find the application of the Word to life.

Christianity is above all community life, ecclesial life in the etymological sense of the word. The Christian belongs to a community. To lose one's awareness of that truth is to betray the spirit of Christ Himself, who lived His faith in the company of His disciples and shared the conditions of the lives of His people. Individualism is incompatible with the spirit of Christ's lifestyle.

"... And the Church is our mother"

Now we are coming to talking about the Church. That is to say, about your mother, according to the Armenian saying.

In our century, we have seen more and more people who believe in God without believing in the Church. In some Catholic countries, like France, for example, statistics show that there is only a small percentage of practicers who fully recognize the authority of the Church.

Do you think that to believe in God it is necessary to believe in the Church?

First of all, I would like to offer two clarifications. The first concerns the statistics. I think that we should not give too much importance to statistics, since life cannot be fully expressed by numbers and figures. There are many phenomena, especially in spiritual life, which cannot be captured in statistics. The second clarification concerns what you just called the "authority of the Church." If that means a power that the clergy exercises over the people, then we are very far from the Christian meaning of authority. There is a deep and even a mystical feeling of the Church's moral authority among many people who do not necessarily sympathize with the hierarchy and the purely institutional power of the Church. I believe that too often, people confuse the notion of the Church with the notion of hierarchy.

The Church, in its orthodox conception, is community. The Christian faith can only be lived in a community; consequently, without a community, there is hardly Christianity, as I just explained. Christianity is not a philosophy. Jesus of Nazareth, its founder, began his mission by establishing a community. Thus the Church is in fact nothing other than that community that tries to live its faith.

Personally, I think that if someone believes in God in an individual manner, and that faith does not succeed in embodying the life of the Church, then that course is only a vision of the world, an intellectual approach, and not Christian faith.

In the beginning of September 1997, the world heard the alarming news of two deaths that happened at the same time. I am referring to the deaths of Mother Theresa and Lady Diana. They were two very different people, and one could say that they were opposites: that small, poor nun and the beautiful princess. Nevertheless, these two women were strongly committed to the poor, the marginalized, the ill, etc. The first was a nun, the other a laywoman who was not particularly linked to an institution-

alized Church. The moral: to do good, you don't need to belong to the Church?

It seems to me that between these two people and these two cases, there is indeed a remarkable difference. Mother Theresa was a person entirely devoted to the service of God; in her, Christ showed Himself to men. Here, I would like to evoke a personal memory that I will always remember: the moment when she came to Armenia. It was during those days of horror that followed the terrible earthquake of Leninakan on December 7, 1988.

As the Catholicos of Cilicia, I had come to Armenia to offer my support and my solidarity to my older brother, the Catholicos of All Armenians Vasken I. I was by his side when Mother Theresa entered his office, accompanied by three sisters. She was already very old and trembled as she walked. The idea that such an elderly and physically weak woman had left everything to travel to the other side of the world to help the disaster victims of our country moved me. She said to Catholicos Vasken: "Holiness, I have neither gold nor silver to offer your victims. But I have three sisters with me who will give their lives entirely to the service of the afflicted, the orphans, the handicapped of your people..." What I would like to say through this example is that it is not service in itself that counts, but the quality of the service, the Christian and authentically human spirit that inspires that service. There are secular organizations for development, for helping the poor or disaster victims. They do a lot and I appreciate them. But I see a qualitative difference when the help is the engagement of an entire life.

You were speaking of Lady Diana. I am delighted by the fact that she did so many charitable works and that she organized acts of goodwill. Fortunately, there are many others who do that, but who go unnoticed in the public because they are not as well known as Diana. I think that her death was extremely regrettable also, because of her youth and the tragic character of her death. But even though every charitable act is good, there is still a difference between ordinary *goodwill* and the *devotion of one's life*. Moreover, I think that service motivated by a transcendent reason, by the love of God, is in itself qualitatively superior.

But there is another aspect to this question. All good comes from God. Thus he who does good deeds makes God present, even if he is not completely aware of it. There is a beautiful expression, I think from Abbé Pièrre, which says: "When you put your hand in the hand of someone in need, you find in his hand the hand of God." Thus someone who does good for others — as much in the material sense as in the moral or spiritual sense — approaches God.

But let's return to the Church: what makes up the Church? The hierarchy? Rites? Liturgy? Once you gave this definition: "The Church is not what we build, but the reality through which we are built ourselves." What does that mean?

The Church is not a human institution, since it was founded by the Son of God. But it is the work of God with man's cooperation, the meeting of God and man. When one participates in a community — which is what the life of the Church means—one is constructed on the inside, spiritually, morally. That is because the action of Christ continues in the Church through the Holy Spirit that constructs us.

When Jesus lived on Earth, He preached with His mouth, He worked with His hands, He accomplished His mission through His actions. Today, we too are composed of His hands, His mouth, His actions... It is in this sense that we always say that the Church is the "mystical body" of Christ.

In the past, people insisted too much on the distinction between *ecclesia docens* and *ecclesia discens*; today we must show that the Church is *one*, composed of laypersons and the clergy together, united by the bond of Christ and by the mystical actions of the Holy Spirit.

Where there are two or three people...

So the Church is not what one understand too often by that word, the hierarchy and the clergy, but rather all the people of God, and, as you just said, the community, the mystical body of the Christ.

Many of the Fathers of the Church based their ecclesiology on two sentences from the Gospel of Matthew: "I am with you always, unto the end of time," and "Where two or three people are gathered in my name, I am among them." Overall, that would mean that the very presence of Christ constitutes the Church. That means that the Church is in the factory, at school, in the bank, at the stadium — everywhere where there are "two or three people" united in His name...

I entirely agree with you. That is why there should not be a break between the Church and social life in all of its forms. That break, that contradiction, is one of the reasons for our crisis today. The Church of Christ is present and acts not only in the institutional churches, but in all of society.

If someone wanted to express in a single Armenian word this idea of the Church as the place where Christ makes Himself present among His disciples, where He descends to Earth, he might say, "Etchmiadzin – since that word means 'the descent of the only Son.'"

You are right. And I would say that since I have lived here in Etchmiadzin, each day, when I am in church and I pray at the altar where, according to our tradition of seventeen centuries, Christ descended from heaven, I think that what is important is not the pious reminiscence of the past. The mystical presence of Christ today takes form in and through our faith, and it works within us. It is in this sense that I often repeat that Etchmiadzin is not primarily a historical monument, but it is a mission, since the presence of Christ for the Christian and the Church signify mission.

"Etchmiadzin is mission" is one of your slogans...

One of the definitions that all Christians give to the Church, in the Creed of Nicaea-Constantinople, says that the Church is One and Holy. However, it is unfortunately not always easy to see the sacredness and the unity of the Church...

The Church, which is a mystery, has two forms in which it exists: the one that is mystical, in the design of Christ, who founded it, and the one that we, who comprise it on Earth, actualize here from that same design. Thus the Church is *one* in the thought and the will of Christ and in our sense of belonging to the same Lord. And in spite of the actual situation of sad and troubling divisions, the unity of the Church still exists. It is a unity of the spirit that makes up the very heart of that sense of belonging to Christ. Unity has not been completely uprooted from the life of the Church, since if that was the case, there would be no Church. It is different for the concrete expression of that unity: as human beings, we all have our faults, our mistakes, which, unfortunately, compromise a large part of our commitment to the Church.

The fact is that in our condition here on Earth, we must not think of what we call the marks of the Church — *one, holy, universal and apostolic* — as a *fait accompli*, but as something to come, a process. *Holy* — yes, the Church is holy, but we who comprise it, we must make our own holiness. Sin is a part of the experience of the Church. All of the Fathers of the Church and the best theologians have had the experience of sin as a challenge to their personal fidelity, but that does not compromise the holiness of the Church. Because that holiness is the very holiness of Christ, who lives in the Church. The light of the sun is always there, even if we cannot see it because of the clouds or our own blindness.

The dialectic between the origin and the mystical nature of the Church on one side, and its condition on Earth on the other, also involves the other epithets. For example, the Church is *apostolic* not only because its origins go back to the apostles; the Church must make itself the bearer of the announcement of Christ from day to day in our modern world. I often say to our bishops and priests that if the Armenian Church calls itself apostolic, it is not only because of the work of the apostles Thaddeus and Bartholomew; we must have the spirit of the apostles within us and we must show it today. It is the same thing for the epithet *catholic*, which means *universal*. Historical circumstances have identified our Church with the Armenian people, but we share with other Christians the universality of the Church, since Christ Himself is not divided between the different denominations!

The crisis

In his letter Redemptoris Missio, *Pope John Paul II speaks of the "great springtime of Christianity" that God is in the process of preparing for the third millennium. You yourself have made similar remarks concerning the future of the Armenian Church.*

However, the churches — and even the Christian faith — in Europe and in what are called the developed countries, seem to be in a state of crisis. The churches are becoming more and more empty, people do not practice the sacraments, many believers do not recognize the authority of the hierarchy, several religious orders are on the path to extinction, their numbers dwindling like those of certain species of seals or Siberian tigers...

One could ask oneself: Is it the churches that have aged, or is it Christianity itself that has aged?

I would not like to make such a strong and clear distinction between the Church and Christianity; for me, Christianity is the incarnation of Christ, which manifests itself in the life of the Church. But that is not the question you are asking.

If the Pope was speaking of a springtime, I also see tangible signs of true renewal in the current conditions of the life of our Church. We are often led to see only negativity everywhere, maybe because of the media. Here I would like to make just one consideration, and I will let you judge it yourself.

If the crisis is so profound, how could we have so many youth movements today in our churches? When I was a young priest, it was those movements that led me toward ecumenism. There were those types of gatherings of young people, particularly in Europe, each year in a new country: the gatherings in Taize, the meetings of young people with the Pope. In August 1997, it was in Paris, with more than a million young participants, and everybody was so deeply impressed by that demonstration and the fact that faith was flourishing among the youth.

The media, being dominated by economic and political factors, does not sufficiently highlight these illustrations of renewal. But there are many dynamic catalysts encouraged by the churches; there are some movements that I have seen in different countries, like the *Focolari* movement. In Italy, I knew the community of Saint-Egidio. In the Orthodox churches, there is the youth movement *Syndesmos*; in the different Protestant denominations there are many other youth groups.... When I see the thousands of young people gathered for these movements, I wonder at what other time in history have there been so many in the life of the Church.

It is true, today churches are often empty. But I remember that when I was a child, the village church was

not always full and the priest complained, at that time
when the church was the very heart of the village....
Personally I am far from considering the number of
followers who attend our liturgical services on Sundays as
a decisive criterion for evaluating the condition of the life
of the Church, or the liveliness of the Christian faith.

What I would like to say is that we must not accord an
absolute value to the signs of indifference toward the
Church in our time. There is indifference and interest at
the same time.

In a recent interview, Cardinal Ratzinger, Prefect of the Congre-
gation for the Doctrine of the Faith — which means guardian of
the Catholic Church — defined the crisis that the churches are
experiencing today as one of the most serious in the history of
Christianity, and that it could only be compared to the
difficulties in the beginning of Christianity (i.e. the persecutions,
the emergence of heretics) or also to the crisis of the sixteenth
century, which gave rise to the Protestant Reformation.

The Cardinal thinks that the Church of the future will be a
minority Church, a small Church. What is your opinion on that
subject?

Not having read Cardinal Ratzinger's interview, I cannot
respond sufficiently. In any case, I think that a lot depends
on our way of relating to reality, of reading the signs of the
times and evaluating events; our approach colors our
interpretation.

As I have already said, statistics cannot explain all of
reality to us. What are the criteria for evaluating the influence of the Church in our world? Is it the number of those

"practicing," of those who go to church on Sundays? But the Church has a mystical presence in people's hearts, even in those who don't go to church. I believe that you said that my father was not "practicing" in the strictest sense of the word; nevertheless, in his family life and at work, he lived in unison with the Church. How do you evaluate someone's affiliation with a Church? Many people who consider themselves non-believers certainly have a kind of spirituality in their lives, inspired by a culture formed in a context of Christian values.

It is true that, especially in the West, society is so secularized that it seems to have excluded the presence of God, which might explain the Cardinal's position. Personally I am not so categorically opposed to secularism, which I see more as a challenge of the times. After all, we live in the world, and if it is true that we Christians are not *of this world*, it is also true that we have been called to live *in the world*, and not outside of society.

I think that, moreover, there are other aspects of the religious situation in Europe and the modern world. I would say that today, secularism has reached a certain saturation. Scientific and technological progress has given men a sense of euphoria, the feeling of being the master of the universe. In this situation, men seem to have swept aside the Creator. But with the progress of science, we have seen that there is no conflict between human knowledge and faith. On the contrary, science has shown us the mystery that is human existence and creation; God the Creator is reclaiming His actuality today in the thoughts and lives of intellectuals and of all those who live their lives in reflection, in the wake of Socrates. I am an optimist and I think that science will allow us to find the feeling that we are not the masters of creation.

Undoubtedly, we are seeing a distancing of the people from religious practice. But personally, I insist that there are promising signs that make me think that in the twenty-first century, there will be more religious life than today. In developed countries, there is a dissatisfaction with the overabundance of material goods; I think that the future will uncover more spiritual values and give a new vigor to faith.

If you look at other religions, especially Judaism and Islam, there also I see signs of a renewal. It is true, here and there, there is also fundamentalism and other extremisms, but it seems to me that the common denominator is still the renewal of religious awareness, of the feeling of God as a Creator and that we are His creatures.

You just mentioned other religions... In Europe, people have the impression that Christianity, even from a cultural point of view, is becoming less and less known. Recently, the Museum of the Louvre was considering organizing courses on religion and rewriting the explanations of many of the exhibited paintings, since the visitors were no longer familiar with the scenes of the Old and New Testament. Nevertheless, even if Christianity on the continent today is not known very well, the thirst for spirituality is very strong. Europeans show a great interest in non-traditional religions, in sects as well as in Eastern spirituality (Zen, Buddhism, yoga).

How do you explain this phenomenon?

I think that non-conformity is an aspect of human life that has always existed. When something becomes traditional, institutionalized, the phenomenon of saturation begins. In the past, as well, this has always been so. People aspire to break out of established structures, to have more personal freedom to express themselves. That quest for liberty is not necessarily opposed to the Church. Churches must take this phenomenon seriously and encourage the birth, within the Church, of less traditional communities and movements. To me, the numerous non-traditional movements born in our time within almost all churches represent a sign of renewal.

It is clear that this spirit of non-conformity might lead to some deviations; I cannot approve of sects that go beyond the bounds of non-conformity. But today, the Church must give more importance to those spontaneous forms of community life.

Also, we must not lose sight of the fact that most of the tendencies that you mentioned will certainly have a very limited duration; the history of the Church has known many movements like the Gnostics of the first century. What counts for the Church now is maintaining its own "freshness."

The challenge of sects

The figures relating to that non-conformity are troubling. In Brazil, a very Catholic country, the free churches create thousands of proselytes. The same phenomenon seems to be pre-occupying Russia, where currently, maybe in a more hasty manner, they are taking measures on the legislative level to thwart the success of foreign missionaries. In the beginning of June

1997, the Armenian Parliament modified the law concerning the freedom of conscience to limit the development of sects. A few months ago, Armenian journalists were talking about around three hundred thousand followers of all kinds of sects in your country.

I think that that information is rather exaggerated. I am not familiar with the situation in Russia or in Brazil, but as for Armenia, the figure that you mentioned seems completely exaggerated to me. You must also look at who these followers are and consider the depth of their convictions. Often these people are pushed by economic reasons or reasons of convenience, by material interests. That is why I think that the "success" of these sects is only a temporary phenomenon in the Armenian context, linked especially to the socio-economic situation of the moment.

All the same, we must not underestimate the risk. The sects are very active; our weakness is a certain passivity. Thus I believe that we have a challenge that we must examine and that will push us to commit ourselves with a new vigor for our Church. Today in Armenia, religious freedom is guaranteed by the Constitution. The Armenian Church is considered the national Church, which is an incontestable historical fact. However, our Church is not privileged by the law. In the new situation of our free state, our Church also has new possibilities of which it must take advantage; thus I am convinced that with more action and energy, it will be able to meet that challenge. As I said in my first official sermon as the one hundred thirty-first Catholicos of All Armenians, it is necessary to bring the Church to life in the lives of the people, so that the people do not feel abandoned or neglected by the

Church and so that they are not tempted to seek their spiritual support elsewhere. What we need is an active, positive pastoral dedication; we need human resources, charisma and action.

So the presence of the sects is a challenge for the Church. That requires, if I have understood correctly, on the one hand, a commitment to the revitalization of the traditional structures of the Church (for example, the parishes, etc.) and on the other, the resort to new, less institutionalized forms of Christian life, like the movements of the laypersons.

Exactly. And in our Armenian Church we have communities of the same kind of movements that you see in Western churches. For example, there is an Armenian movement called the Spiritual Fraternity. Their center is in Yerevan, and they have branches in the other dioceses, as well as in the diaspora. They organize Bible study and prayer meetings with religious chants in modern Armenian and liturgical hymns in the classic language. They are a part of the Armenian Church, while keeping the autonomy of their organization as an association of followers. I think that these forms of associated Christian life, not very institutionalized, are a response to the challenge of the sects.

You do not seem to be pessimistic regarding the future of the Church, even when it concerns the troublesome problem of the sects...

I am not pessimistic; I think that you cannot be Christian without being optimistic. God is not only all-powerful, but He is also all-merciful.

Also, an error that we Christians commit rather frequently is that we idealize the past; we forget that in history, there were always times when the Church was refused or rejected. Atheism is not a product of our times, and the sects and deviations have always existed, from the time of the apostles. But the life of the Church has continued in spite of everything.... There is a very precise reason for this: the constant presence of Christ in the heart of the Church. He promised us: "I am with you always, unto the end of time."

❧ CHAPTER VI ❧

The Church:
Its Internal Life

What is authority?

Next to the problem of the loss of followers that we discussed, the Church must, on one hand, face a series of problems regarding its internal life, and on the other, confront the expectations and challenges of the modern world. We are going to speak about some of the internal problems in the life of the Church.

In all Christian churches, but especially the oldest ones (the Eastern churches and the Roman Catholic Church), the concept of authority is fundamental. In most modern languages, this term comes from the Latin auctoritas, *derived from the noun* auctor – author, he who produces something. *People call an author an artist who creates a work in this or that genre, but also, there is God, the Author of life...*

What is authority in the Church?

In my personal conception, authority in the Church is not quite the etymological meaning that you have underlined, since it makes one think of the created work as belonging to its creator, whereas every authority in the Church has a representative character. A bishop is not the head of a local Church; he is only a vicar, the person representing the leader of the Church, who is Christ. A bishop has not appropriated that authority; it is the Church that has chosen him and sent him for that service. In other words, that authority comes from the Church.

Moreover, in our conception of Eastern churches, authority is *conciliar*: it is the totality of the Church, through the Council, that exercises supreme authority.

In the Gospel, Jesus had an absolute, divine authority; He chose, shaped and then sent out His disciples. In doing so, He gave them very precise directives, as we can see this in the beginning of Chapter Nine of the Gospel of Saint Luke; that is the delegation of authority. Authority in the Church comes from Christ and manifests itself in the evidence of the successors of the apostles. Since we are all weak and sinners, authority without humility and without service is opposed to Jesus' command. Thus, the criterion for the authenticity of authority is humility, the quality of the service and the loyalty to Christ of the person who exercises it.

Authoritarianism and anarchy

One of the tests that the disciples had to face during the life of Jesus was the test of power. You know the episode in the gospels where the disciples discussed who was the greatest among them. At that moment, Jesus offered them a new conception of authority: "The leaders of the gentiles order them as masters, and the powerful make them feel their power. But that must not happen among you. On the contrary: if one of you wishes to be great, he must be a servant, and if one of you wishes to be first, then he must be your slave...." These words seem to clearly

condemn authoritarianism, the confusion of authority and
power. Christ Himself had already overcome the temptation of
power in the desert. Finally, at the Last Supper, while washing
the apostles' feet, Jesus gave them a concrete example of this
authority-in-service.

Do you think that this new concept of authority is truly fol-
lowed in the Church? In fact, one often has the impression that
within the Church, there are problems relating to relationships of
power, the domination of those who have authority over their
subordinates, the abuse of power, careerism, etc.

We should not generalize; in the Church, like everywhere
in the world, there are very distinct cases, and ways of
exercising authority that are more or less evangelical. For
me, the source of the conception of authority comes from
the pages of the Gospel that you quoted. Authority in the
Church has nothing to do with power in the political
world; it is of a different quality. In society, the person
who, in one way or another, appropriates or obtains power
must try to keep his position; for a servant of God,
authority must never become authoritarianism. Why do
we have this authority? What is its goal? It is service to
others: "I have not come to be served, but to serve," says
Jesus.

There are people in the Church who use their authority
for themselves. I cannot really accept that. I believe in
authority, in the authority that comes from Christ and that
is service. It is for that reason that I can accept neither
anarchy nor authoritarianism, whether in the sense of the
monopolization of a privilege for one's sole profit, or in the
sense of a degeneration of authority into absolute, despotic
power. Especially in the Middle Ages, the Church often

exercised authority in the same way as the powers of this world, and today, we still see the consequences of that use of authority.

Anarchism is also a deviation from the just use of authority, and is in some ways the opposite tendency of authoritarianism. A rather frequent error is the claim that there is no authority in the Church. All of Jesus' life shows us that He had a great authority, even though He exercised it in His own way; Christ founded the college of the apostles, and entrusted His authority to them. So the Church recognizes authority, but an authority qualitatively different than that of this world.

In the sermon of your installation as the Supreme Patriarch of All Armenians, you talked about authority in the Church in conjunction with these two expressions of Christ: "to take the yoke" and "to bear the cross." What did you mean?

I thought of the authority given to me by that election as a duty, and not as a privilege, nor as a recognition of my possible qualities.

When Jesus said, "Take up the cross and follow me," that means that one cannot follow Him without taking up the cross. But the cross is service to others. The sins that Christ took upon Himself were the sins of others.

In my life, there were times when I felt clearly that the cross, which I had to bear like every Christian, was getting heavier. The first moment was my ordination as a deacon; then the sacerdotal ordination; the day when I was made a bishop; and finally, when I became Catholicos, first of Cilicia, then of All Armenians. On each of these occasions,

I felt that the same cross was becoming heavier and heavier... Finally, two years ago, I really felt it as a yoke, that is, an extreme duty, as if I was giving myself limitlessly in total devotion. There, too, I think that authority is proportional to the extent to which one gives of oneself. It is in this sense that I feel the weight of Jesus' words: "My yoke is easy, and my burden light" (Mt 11:30).

The lesson of Pontius Pilate

Another aspect of the problem of authority and power is careerism. Careerism does not only mean a readiness to compromise one's conscience for one's ambition, but also to put one's career above all other values.

There is something that strikes me each time I reread the story of the Passion of Jesus in the Gospels: the character of Pontius Pilate. He was a complete stranger to the case he had to judge, and was known to be violent. But from the first moment, the Galilean whom he found before him inspired compassion, maybe even sympathy. Contrary to his own habits, he did everything he could to save the defendant; he tried with all of his means, played all his cards, tried every recourse of his oratory and histrionic skills.... He did not stop until he realized that his career was at stake. The argument of the leaders of the priests who made him surrender was: "If you release this man, you are not a friend of Caesar..."

The passion of Christ, the highpoint of the story of salvation, seems to tell us that power in its different manifestations is really the strongest temptation...

First, I would like to repeat a remark that I have already stated in the course of our interviews: careerism for me is an aberration of authority. I just said that authority has a value in the extent to which it is service; careerism is the *cult* of authority. To my understanding, in my conception of Christian morality, careerism is one of the gravest sins.

What you are saying regarding Pontius Pilate is very fair: as a man of the law, he saw that Jesus had done no wrong. But he lacked courage since he thought of authority in terms of his career and not of service. He wanted to maintain his position, to have the advantages of his post, the pride of his dignity. At the moment of his choice, his career won out over justice, truth. His great question— "What is truth?"—was not for him an intellectual interrogation, nor a question of life. The supreme value for Pilate was his well-being, his position, his prestige.

How many new Pontius Pilates do we have? Unfortunately, there are many of them, even in the Church...

Careerism, monks and the married episcopate

In Eastern churches, next to the celibate clergy, composed primarily of monks, there is also a married clergy. As the bishops and all the hierarchs of the Church are chosen only among monks, these monks seem to be very concerned by the temptation of careerism, which is not the case for the married priests who cannot make a career of it. In the opinion of some Orthodox, the ambition of an eventual ecclesiastical career probably provokes a certain number of monastic "vocations," which could lead to a deterioration of monasticism.

Regarding this problem, some people would like to return to a married episcopate. What do you think?

You see, the temptation of careerism does not only concern monks, but exists in all men. It seems to me that that temptation does not depend on a person's situation, nor on his rank. It is rather a question of the conception of authority, and also of character...

As for a married episcopate, as you know, there are no dogmatic prohibitions, since in the first centuries there were married bishops. However, since then, the Church has preferred to select its hierarchs from among the monks, and we must respect that evolution in the Church.

I have been a monk and priest for thirty-five years. Being the Catholicos now, I have passed through all the levels of authority in the Church. What I have seen is that the function of a diocesan bishop is such a heavy charge, it seems to me that it would be difficult to reconcile it with a family life. In our Church, a bishop, particularly in the diaspora, is not only responsible for the spiritual life of the diocese, but he also has social responsibilities as the head of the Armenian community; for example, the Armenian schools of his region are entrusted to him. That involves a number of obligations that go beyond his spiritual ministry. A person who assumes such a duty must be free from family responsibilities, which, among others things, have become more onerous than they were before.

I am convinced that people benefit from our tradition of both married and single clergy members. But there is a difference between these two kinds of vocation. The celibate priest must engage in prayer and intellectual, educational and administrative service. The married priest is engaged primarily in the parish, in the pastoral service directly related to the everyday lives of his people. If he is married, then he understands much better than a monk the different aspects of family life, the problems that couples face, children, etc. That is why in our tradition the priest must normally be married. These two different realizations of the same vocation are complementary and, for that reason, should not be confused.

But there is another aspect of this problem that was not mentioned in your question and that I would like to stress. If we understand the ecclesiastical ministry as a service, then it is the quality of that service that gives authority to a priest or a bishop. I have seen more than a few cases in which a married priest had much more authority in his community than his bishop. Thus I believe that in this problem, we must not look at the rank or the hierarchical position, since real authority depends on the quality of the service one offers.

Authority for life

"The Church is the mystical body of Jesus Christ," the catechism reminds us. At the same time, from the human perspective, the Church is a community of people with very precise hierarchical relationships. At the head of many churches, there is a group of directors, who, in many cases, have a position for life, which is also your personal situation. Many sociologists and psychologists think that a person holding power for an extended period of time creates a sort of imbalance in that person. In fact, it is very difficult for a person who is in power for a long time to not make his opinions, tastes, etc., absolute.

Many religious orders of the Catholic Church have had the bitter experience of finding themselves on the path to extinction because of the abuses of power of those who have been in authority too long. In our times, banks, factories, and businesses

try to change their directing personnel as often as possible. Why
do churches keep their hierarchs in positions of authority for life?

I cannot judge for the other churches, but I can speak res-
ponsibly from my own knowledge about the Armenian
Church. Except for the Catholicos, we have no hierarch in
a position for life. Our bishops in certain dioceses (in the
United States, for example) are elected for a term of four or
seven years, and then the elections are repeated. The
bishops who are not reelected keep their episcopal title,
because of their consecration, but they no longer exercise
its administrative functions, or they go to another diocese.
So the problem of exercising authority for too long is not as
serious as it is in the Catholic Church or in other Orthodox
churches. In the past, bishops were elected in one diocese
and were bishops for life; however, they could step down
themselves, or be removed by churchgoers, which has
happened several times. The body of people responsible
for the bishop's election could put an end to his term,
which, obviously, did not mean the end of their rank or
episcopal charisma.

As for the Catholicos, being the head of the Church, he
is the guardian of the faith. He must guarantee fidelity to
traditions and to the orthodoxy of the faith. For the
people, the Catholicos is the shepherd of the Church and
the spiritual father of the nation. That is why he is elected
for life. However, there have been cases, here at Holy
Etchmiadzin as well as in the Catholicossate of Cilicia,
where the Catholicos, for health reasons or other obstacles,
asked to be replaced. Thus, after the election of a new
Catholicos, the former Catholicos retires while keeping the
dignity of the Catholicos. The newly elected one takes on

the full responsibility of the Church during the life of the former...

...which was the case for you during your first six years in the See of Cilicia.

Yes. That situation is not infrequent in the history of our Church.

A democratic church?

The Catholic and the Orthodox churches are structured like a monarchy or an aristocracy. Such institutions no longer exist in most modern countries, or remain only as a vestige of the past.
Could you envision the existence of a "democratic" Church?

People often speak of the Armenian Church as a democratic church. Personally, I am not inclined to apply such sociological categories to the life of the Church. The Church is neither a state nor a parliament, and we don't make decisions in it with votes; of course, on the administrative end, that is how we resolve problems. But the Christian faith, its preaching and its application to everyday life are not things that can be put in relation to the duty a state has to perform its own functions, since the exercising of authority in the Church is not a duty but a vocation. The sacred character of the Church must always remain intact because—let us never forget—the Church is the sacrament of sacraments.

Also, in my opinion, the parallel that you are drawing with the different social systems is not sufficient, since monarchies in our times are no more than a symbol of national unity, whereas in our Church, a priest or patriarch's authority is real.

I would also add that in the Armenian Church, laypeople actively participate, particularly in administrative, economic and other tasks. So the absolutism of monarchies has no place in the Church. In any case, you cannot make decisions concerning faith, dogma, liturgy or spirituality through a democratic process; when you are dealing with eternal truths, it is not a question of a majority or a minority...

Laymen and the selection of the hierarchy

In the Armenian Church, laymen also participate in the election of the Catholicos. He is elected by an assembly of representatives from all Armenian communities, made up, in large part, of laypeople...

Generally in a ratio of two-thirds laymen.

As for the bishops, in the past they were elected by a diocesan assembly that was six-sevenths laypeople. How are they chosen today?

The case that you mentioned is quoted by the Patriarch Malachia Ormanian in his work on the Armenian Church and involved the Armenians who lived in the Ottoman Empire, dependent upon the Patriarchate of Constantinople. In 1863, a constitution fixed that proportion to six-sevenths laymen and one-seventh clergymen for the electoral body, called the National Assembly, which elected the bishops and the Patriarch. The massive presence of laymen was due to the fact that the Patriarch was the center of national Armenian life in the Ottoman Empire; he was involved in affairs concerning education, civil rights, social work, etc. In the rest of the Church, it was different. Here at Etchmiadzin, after the Russian imperial conquest of Armenia, the Catholicossate was under the power of the czars. The czars created a constitution concerning our Church that regulated the election of the Catholicos and bishops. The Electoral Assembly, which was also made up of a majority of laypeople (but not six-sevenths), elected two candidates and the czar chose one.

Today the election of bishops is handled through two systems. In certain dioceses of the diaspora, the bishop is elected by the Diocesan Assembly, which in the Catholicossate of Cilicia is composed of six-sevenths laymen. In the dioceses of the diaspora under the jurisdiction of the Catholicossate of All Armenians, the composition of the assembly varies from place to place, according to the by-laws of each diocese. So in the dioceses of Armenia and other countries of the former Soviet Union, since there was no body formed by the Church, the bishops are chosen by the Catholicos.

The people of God

In the Catholic Church, and maybe even more in Orthodox churches, one perceives a certain distance between the people and the clergy, the same distance that once separated the aristocrats and the people. However, the Church says that it is above all the "people of God." How can the people participate more in the life of the Church?

As you just said, it is the people who make up the Church; the clergy and the hierarchy must be in the service of its followers. You know that according to Saint Peter's first epistle (1 Pt 2:9), all of the people of God participate in the priesthood. The distance to which you refer is thus a deviation, the product of a bad historical evolution that has no reason to exist.

I think that the Armenian Church has been able to remain the Church of the people, a Church in the service of the nation. The clergy has never been a caste; the priest is, in general, a member of the local community. That is why the clergy in our Church may be closer to the people than in some other churches. Presently, the participation of the people in the life of the Church seems satisfactory to me. In the different sectors of responsibility and service in our Church, we have people, men and women, who are actively engaged at the level of the parish, the diocese and even the Catholicossate. Particularly in educational and charitable services, the people are at the forefront; catechism, to a large degree, is in the hands of women. As for the people's participation in the selection of hierarchs, we have already spoken about that.

Obviously, there is still much for us to do. For example, the participation of the people in liturgical life. Liturgy is a communal prayer *par excellence*; so everyone's participation is essential. It will take some time, but I think that we will get there.

The most sensitive creatures

In the meditations on the Via Crucis, *which you wrote for the Pope on the occasion of Good Friday 1997, you say:*

> *In Bethlehem, Jesus opened His eyes to the light and saw His mother first. At Golgotha, His eyes closed on the image of His mother. Thus, His mother was the first and the last thing in His thoughts and concerns, in His love and His considerations. Women: the most sensitive creatures to come from the hand of God; His daughters, our mothers and sisters. They were closest to the Lord, sworn to His mission, participants in His agony, His anguish, His sadness.*

What is woman to you?

A being of God, who participates in life with the unique qualities that God gave her. In my understanding, the role of the woman is expressed in a sublime manner in the image of the Mother of God. The sensitivity that I was talking about in the meditation that you quoted is one of the feminine qualities, and maternity also occupies a central place. Women are inclined to express love (for their children, for example) in terms of a solicitude that words cannot express. The woman with these qualities, which should never be cast aside, has an extremely important role in human life; as a mother, she plays a fundamental role in the formation of a child's personality. In our times, with influences and pressures exerted on young generations so much stronger than they were in the past, the mother's role is becoming even more important.

The Mother of God was already so loved and venerated during her life on Earth by the apostles and then by the first generation of Christians because she was the most exemplary manifestation of maternity. The role of mother is determinant for women, and to speak of her social emancipation without considering it would be to betray her nature and vocation. I have already quoted our Catholicos Karekin Hovsepian, who said that the family is a church whose priest is the mother...

Women, the priesthood and the diaconate

In Graz on June 24, 1997, you gave a press conference, seated between two women: Chiara Lubich, founder of Focolari, *and Hlope Brigalia Bam, secretary general of the SACC, the South African Council of Churches. On that occasion, you yourself did not fail to remark to the journalists: "Who would have imagined fifty years ago that a Catholicos or a Patriarch would be seated at a table at a theological conference between two women!"*

In the West, people talk about the role of women in the Church. The Synod of the Church of England accepted the priesthood of women on November 11, 1992. It was a critical moment for the Anglican Church: several Anglican priests asked to join the Catholic Church while others turned toward the Orthodox Church.

What do you think of allowing women priests?

Women should not be subject to discrimination in society or in the Church. But that does not mean that we should neglect or blur the difference between men and women, since that difference leads to creation, and we must respect it. This distinction does not mean discrimination. As for the priesthood, in the life and teachings of Christ, the ministry was entrusted to men. So I think that it is necessary to respect what the Lord has passed onto us. The tradition of the Church goes directly back to Christ. So it is not acceptable, in my opinion, to change that tradition today.

This tradition cannot be understood through sociological considerations, by saying that in the time of Jesus, women did not have the position in society that they do now. It is very important to note that in many cases, Jesus went against the grain of his time. If we go in this direction, then all of Christ's teaching can be questioned and we would fall into the temptation of relativism. The Church's doctrine cannot be dictated by the sociological thought of this or that era; the Church is the guardian of tradition, which Saint Paul frequently stressed in his epistles. So we either follow the lessons of Christ as they are, or we construct a religion that might be rational, that follows social customs, but that does not have much to do with absolute truth.

Apart from the aspect of the priesthood, I think that women must play a large role in the life of the Church since the service that they can provide is important and unique and does not have to do with the priesthood. The priesthood is not all that there is in the life of the Church...

One of the arguments of people who do not accept women priests, which you just mentioned, is that there were no woman priests in the apostolic era, in the first century, or in the times of the Fathers. However we know that in the primitive Church, there were deaconesses, who are present today in Protestant denominations and who existed within the Orthodox Church until the eleventh century. Could you imagine the Orthodox churches reinstituting these deaconesses?

I think so, since it was present in tradition. In our Church we had deaconesses until recently. I personally remember three deaconesses who had come from Constantinople to our seminary in Antelias when I was a young priest.

How did they exercise their position? Did they provide only a social service, such as taking care of the poor or sick people of the community?

No. They were also involved in liturgical service. I remember that they would serve at the altar of the church, reading the Gospel, presenting offerings, preparing the incense. Those are the prerogatives of the diaconate, which they received with the ordination of the Armenian Patriarch of Constantinople.

The institution of the female diaconate since then has been neglected. But if people wanted to reestablish it, there would not be any canonical obstacles. Personally, I would be ready to do so when practical conditions permit.

Woman and sacredness

In all churches, even in those where there are no female priests, women make up a large majority of practicers. Recently an American Catholic publicist began a campaign to defend "men's rights" in the Catholic Church, which, he thought, was too "feminized." Why do women go to Church more than men?

I have thought very much about that problem. However, I think that God might have endowed women with a particular sensibility for spiritual values, for love. Men, who have always been concerned with earning enough to support their families, are more withdrawn and absorbed by their careers and involvement in society, whereas women are more oriented toward spiritual life, prayer. My impression is that women are more inclined toward spirituality.

If I understand correctly, there is, let's say, a sociological side (the fact that men have always been more involved with work), but there is also a psychological *and* spiritual *side. Could someone say that women are more welcoming toward what is sacred because of their psycho-physiological composition, which makes them capable of "welcoming life" in the spiritual sense as well as from a physiological point of view?*

Precisely. I think that that can be explained by that sensibility inherent in women's nature. That is something that is difficult to prove scientifically, but of which I am convinced with the experience of my years, seeing women's engagement in spiritual life.

The feminine genius and the "weaker sex"

In the history of the Church in this century, two women played very important roles without exercising a sacerdotal ministry; I am referring to Mother Theresa and Chiara Lubich. They had worldwide renown, were personally close with the popes, and consultants for the synods of the bishops. Most importantly, they helped millions of their contemporaries open themselves to

God; and they were very close to each other. Recently, after Mother Theresa's death, several journalists interviewed Chiara Lubich, asking questions about the "feminine genius" and the role of women in the Church. And here is one of her answers: "The feminine genius resides in a characteristic that Mary had: she was not invested in a ministry, but she was invested in love, in charity, which is the greatest gift, the most exemplary charisma that comes from heaven. Thus was Mother Theresa."

Holiness, what is the feminine genius for you?

The investment of love of which Chiara Lubich speaks, that consecration through love, that is something that is very right. What I was saying about the sensibility for spirituality inherent to women might be a synonym for that idea of consecration through love. You are asking me to define the feminine genius; I think that the answer is in your question, when you cite those two women completely devoted to God without having received a sacerdotal ministry. I would like to say that there is a "vocation of love," which can be attained by every human being but which is something very particular in women. A woman who gives herself entirely to God and to His service is already consecrated by the love of God.

I am delighted by Chiara Lubich's statement and it seems to me to be well founded, both for Mother Theresa and for other women who have left an indelible mark on Christian history. It is something that transcends our logic and our institutional structures. God can never be contained in such structures, in the same way that you cannot contain the rays of the sun. And, in our times, the two women that you mentioned are among those who have shone the most brightly and truly.

One thing that always strikes me in the story of the Passion of Christ in the gospels is that from the moment of Jesus' arrest, He makes a very clear distinction between the men and women among His disciples. The apostles abandoned the Lord, while the women stayed close to Him. That might be why He first showed Himself to the women disciples upon His return.

The Gospel seems to put the idea of women as the "weaker sex," which is seen in many languages, into question...

In a certain sense, the same is true for the Armenian Church. The first martyr of our Church was a woman, Saint Sandoukht, the daughter of King Sanatrouk, who had been converted to Christianity by the apostle Saint Thaddeus. Women have had a great influence on the formation of our Church; the saints Hripsime, Gayane, Mariane and thirty-two others were at the very origin of Armenia's conversion to Christianity. Saint Gregory, after being freed from prison, saw that his first duty was to honor the martyrs...who were all women!

In addition to that, we have other great female figures in the history of our Church. In the beginning of the fourth century, two other women played an essential role in Armenia's conversion to Christianity: Queen Ashkhen, and the King Tiridates's sister, Khosrovitoukht. In the fifth century, the wives of the feudal princes, "well raised and of a sumptuous allure," according to Yeghishé, the historian of that period, organized a revolt against the men, who, before the battle of Avarayr, had renounced the Christian faith before the King of Kings of Persia and accepted Mazdeism. Their revolt had a major influence in the Armenian resistance against the Persian's attempts to restore Mazdeism. Toward the end of the same century, there was another important woman of our Golden Age, Tzovig, a lady of the nobility, who supervised the young princes' education and raised them in the Christian faith.

Throughout history, the respective churches have known a number of female personalities who paved the way and sowed the seeds of the Christian faith. You see very clearly that in our experience, women cannot truly be defined as the "weaker sex."

The Church and young people

I would like to talk about young people now, about their expectations, their place in the Church. Have you often had to deal with young people in you pastoral work?

Yes, very often. I would even say constantly. From the beginning of my ministry, I have had the opportunity to take care of young people. To clarify, the serving of young people, in the seminary and at university, was the very beginning of my work as a young priest in Lebanon. In fact, in 1963, I formed the Association of Armenian University Students, which was composed of male and female students from different universities in Lebanon and still exists today. Throughout these last decades, it helped form the personalities of many remarkable Armenians who are now all over the world. When I see them, they often tell me that the time they spent together with other university youths solidified their commitment to the Church and to society in different countries of the diaspora.

At this moment in Armenia, we are doing pastoral work with young people, which is very promising for the future of our Church. They have organized a Christian association which also works inside Yerevan State University. They have a chaplain and work in collaboration with the recently established College of Theology.

How do you view these young people?

The youth are not a class, and must not be considered as a category which participates in a certain proportion in this or that aspect of society or the Church. They are people who demonstrate vivacity, an inclination toward action. In short, what they are to me is not an issue of age, but a state of mind, a quality of life. Youth is that way of acting with enthusiasm, vigor, effervescence and commitment that we must consider a very important force in the Church.

Youth has always been synonymous with optimism, vigor, enthusiasm; you add to those terms the word "commitment." However, today, people often say that young people have neither models nor ideals, that they have no goals, they are dedicated to nothing, they don't face the challenges of life... That might explain the distance between young people and the Church. Also, the Church, with its slow pace and thousand-year-old rites, its difficult symbolism, might seem out of date to young people. What place can young people have in the Church?

I do not think that we should generalize about the passivity of young people today. People often say that the youth of today is lost. Personally, I believe that there are enough young people in our churches today, but that often, their contribution goes unrecognized. I see that there is a new awareness among the youth of their place in the Church.

What counts is their awareness, since we are not heads of churches who have to dictate the place of young people! Let's let them realize that they have a responsibility, and that they have to find the way to deal with that responsibility themselves. It is important to let them arrive at certain decisions and forms of commitment themselves. It is a mistake to think that we must prepare everything for them. In my opinion, we must do everything to give them the opportunity to cultivate their willingness to assume those responsibilities within themselves. The young rich man who presented himself to Christ realized by himself that he was missing something. Unfortunately, before Jesus' proposition, he did not have enough courage or will.

I have said that youth for me is the courage to face challenges, and to not let them escape. It is in the nature of young people to want to change things, even things that have always been considered unchangeable. If there is that kind of determination among young people, then I think that they will find the means to overcome all obstacles and to bring that breath of fresh air that the churches need. In a word, we must have confidence in our youth.

Do you think that the churches must also take a step toward young people?

Yes, certainly. What the Church has done until now is not enough. There is still much to do. But there are promising signs. I think that the youth is essential to the life of the Church. What is important is that the Church recognizes that young people are a singular gift.

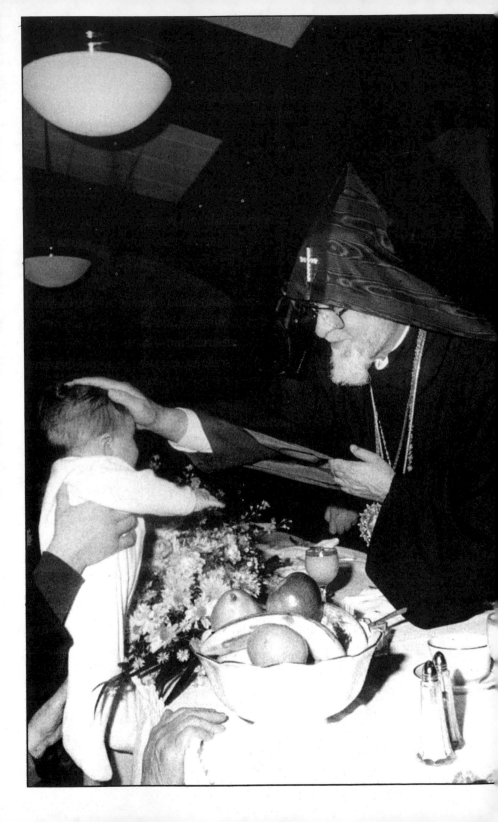

CHAPTER VII

Human Love, Family & Sexuality

What is human love?

All of the churches talk about love: supernatural *love, for which the first Christians adopted certain words (in Greek,* agape, *and in Latin,* caritas) *in order to distinguish it from human love.*

...But there is also human love, which all men and women have experienced. What is the mystery of affection, the disposition of sentiments that makes us feel an inclination toward another person, for whom we are ready to forget ourselves? Is the attraction that one person feels for another an instinct that God created for the continuation of our species and, for that reason, is not different from any animals' instincts? Or is there something more, something that has to do with the very essence of God, which we call love?

Love is God's influence. The classification of the different expression of that love in human and social life is purely conventional. But love remains one: it is the blossoming of a human being, or, as the Bible says, the image of God is love.

Love toward another human being comes from God, not only for the purpose of procreation, but for sharing the human condition that God gave us. The family is not, so to speak, a "machine for procreation"; it is primarily a home, a community of life and sharing. Human love is not only a physical relationship; it has a deeply spiritual dimension. Love, the source of all human happiness, has different manifestations: love between a man and a woman, love between generations, love for our friends and relatives. One of its manifestations is love towards another person with the goal of creating a family and realizing a profound and full communion with spiritual and physical elements.

That physical expression of love, the sexual act between a man and a woman, is the total and reciprocal gift of oneself. That is certainly a religious concept! What is sexuality from the Church's perspective?

It is what you just stated: an act of a physical nature, in the context of the sharing of the entire lives of two people who want to create a home in which love is shared with everyone. The goal of a family is not only to physically give life, that is to say, to create children; rather, the goal is to create an environment in which the members of the family can truly flourish and attain happiness. The family is the center of human life, the accomplishment of God's act of creation. It is not about a contract between two people, but of a state of life that God has dictated to us since His creation of man and woman, and where we find complete happiness.

Sexuality and the family

So you see both procreation and human sexuality in general as being oriented toward the family. However, you certainly know that in our day and age, on the contrary, there are many factors that have led to a new vision of sexuality: the pace of life in the industrialized age, stress, the exaltation of violence in the media. Sexuality is seen and experienced as a safety valve, an escape in a life full of stress and frustrations. Sex today is a product, and although in the history of humans, the body has always been bought and sold (since people say that prostitution is the oldest profession in the world), in our times sex is a booming industry that sells all kinds of emotions, always more and more artificial. That is the case with pornography via the telephone or the Internet.... That means that sexuality is no longer exclusively linked to the concept of family, and not necessarily linked to the human body. Within families also, sexuality is often experienced in an unhealthy way: the extremely high incidence of incest and the sexual abuse of minors within families is proof of that...

What is the attitude of the churches regarding this problem?

Not being a sociologist, I cannot give you a detailed explanation that would be the result of specific research. So I will only tell you my point of view, as a simple observation. In my opinion, the family crisis has three causes.

First, the educational system. Schools today should not only impart information concerning the different areas of knowledge, as is generally and unfortunately the case. They should teach the ability to establish relationships with others. The absence of such a "moral education" is one of the causes of the weakening of our sense of family.

A second cause is the media. Personally, I think that there are still many good families today, but television, newspapers and other media only offer us exceptionally perverted situations. In doing so, they encourage all kinds of deviations and present the exceptions as the rule. The place and the role of the family in society are misunderstood or ignored by the media. In the United States, particularly in less urban areas, I saw that family is still a very strong value. I think that the media, if only to be objective, should show us examples of healthy families.

Third, I think that churches are partially responsible because they have not oriented preaching toward the lives of the people. Too often, we talk and write about theological issues that are rather removed from real life and the problems that concern people from day to day. We are not meeting our task of raising people's awareness, and of allowing that awareness, formed in the Christian faith, to orient itself toward the application of the principles of Christian morality with the freedom that God gave to every man.

"That is why a man will leave his father and mother and cleave to his wife, and the two will be one flesh," says Jesus Christ in His discourse about marriage (Mt 19:5). To be one flesh is the greatest experience of unity between two individuals on Earth, since it would mean being a single person. Why should that experience only be possible within the family? What would you say to a man and woman who love each other sincerely but do not want to make a definitive commitment?

I would say that if there is such a love between the two, then their bond does not exist for only a short time. It demands an eternal commitment because authentic love is never conditional. Jesus says that they will be one flesh, an experience of true sharing, a communion of love, the feeling of being one in the other. Obviously, there are distinctions and differences between men and women, between the roles of one and the other, and that unity of flesh does not erase those differences...

Overall, Jesus says that the two must not only reproduce (which Genesis had already ordered), but that they must unite themselves in an inseparable bond. That is why I do not believe in the idea of a "temporary family." That would be making the family a kind of merchandise, denying the very idea of family, which is an integral part of God's creation.

Divorce

After the sentence we have just spoken about, Jesus says that man must not separate that which God has united (Mt 19:6). However, divorce is a very common practice today, and is allowed by the Orthodox churches...

When he says that man must not separate what God has united, Jesus Himself also gives us an exception: adultery. Our churches of the East have accepted divorce based on that lesson of Jesus. Aside from adultery, there are specific cases that are cited in our canonical law in which the Church must see if the couple's communion truly exists, if it is irreparably broken. It is only in these particular cases that the Church grants divorces.

I personally think that our churches must be more strict than they are now in the examination of cases and in the handling of divorces.

By saying that, you are going completely against the grain. In fact, you certainly know that, for example, in the Catholic Church, many faithful Catholics believe that the Church should be more understanding and tolerant concerning divorce...

I am not speaking for all Orthodox churches. When I talk about being more strict, I mean that before granting a divorce we should do everything possible to save the marriage and the family: take care of people, advise them to wait a little while, a year or more, and make every effort to work towards a reconciliation. In my pastoral practice, I have seen many times that some people who request a divorce, after some time of pastoral work on the part of priests and well-educated laypeople, go back on their decision and rebuild their family.

So it is not a question of a severity that is indifferent to these couples' problems and their sometimes tragic situations. I simply mean that it is good to take some time to think carefully, and to do some pastoral work with the goal of reconstituting the family. We must use all means to make divorce a limited exception.

The modern tendency to which you are alluding is marked by an extremely liberal and permissive approach. That poses a danger that could undermine our society — and that we must avoid and fight at any cost.

Monks and love

At the age of twenty, you made a rather difficult and important decision: to follow the monastic path. What is the experience of human love for a person who has renounced his family for God? What experience does a monk have with affection, tenderness, delicacy? Some think that a Church led by monks cannot understand human love; others, on the contrary, think that only monks know the secret of love...

I think that for a monk, his love toward people can cover the highest manifestations of love. Monks have given themselves to God, who is the source of all love. The love that he shows for his neighbor, his community, the people he serves, fills his life.

I can say that in my personal experience, I felt that I was a full person in the act of giving to others, in my total—my friends even say "relentless"—devotion to the service of the people. For example, when I was a rector of the seminary, I cared for my students in a way that gave me full satisfaction.

As you just said in your question, there are so many expressions of love that a monk can fill his life with committed service, comprised of attention, delicacy, generosity, finesse.... That monk will have the satisfaction of having passed on to others what God gave him: serenity of spirit, a solicitude without reserve toward others. I can say that I have had the experience of spiritual paternity with my students. When I was a diocesan bishop, educational and social services were an important dimension in my life, and I learned how love can manifest itself through clerical and educational action in the context of a community, which is a family.

I am thus convinced that a monk can be a master, an educator of love, through the quality and intensity of his service to others. Let us not forget that love, after all, is the cross. If you do not bear the cross, if you are not capable of forgetting yourself for others and suffering for them, that is when you do not have the experience of what love is...

People often say that today, in our secularized society, a choice like chastity or virginity is not possible — it is an anachronism.

Why are you saying "today"? Man has always been as he is today, and chastity in the past was as difficult as it is in our time. But if those things were possible in the past for men like us, then why shouldn't they exist now? I think that it is commonplace to justify our weaknesses with the faults and conditions of life in "modern times." Although society has changed, human beings are always the same, and in all of the history of the Church, where chastity is concerned, we have had many cases of failure and weakness, but just as many cases of heroic victory. In short, chastity depends primarily on the person and not on social conditions. Fidelity to a vow of chastity has always been difficult, and in making that vow, you accept that difficulty; otherwise, your commitment is not serious, worthy or true.

Jesus says that the phenomenon of people who do not get married can by explained by different reasons: for some, it is a question of an impossibility since their birth; others are made incapable of it by men; others choose not to marry for the Kingdom of Heaven. Then He adds a rather enigmatic expression, which seems to say that not everyone can understand this choice (Mt 19:11-12). So there is a mystery involved. But for you, as someone who has made this choice, what does it mean?

I perceive it as a vocation, as the reason for my existence. In accepting this choice, I have accepted my life's goal, the service to God realized through the service to others. This vocation is a renouncement of oneself — without denying one's identity — through the sharing with other people of the abilities, talents, service and love that God has given us. Through serving these people, others cease to be "others" for you and become members of your community, your "family," the family of God.

You relate the personal choice of dedicating one's life to God to service to men. That means that monasticism, a sort of abandonment of the world and of temptations, is, however, related to society.

Absolutely. Even a solitary hermit in the desert, even the strictest anchorites, who do nothing but pray, are linked to society for the sole reason that they are praying for the people. And if you take the case of Saint Anthony, the first Desert Father, the founder of monasticism in Egypt, you see that he was not altogether alone. He used to visit the people. Detaching oneself from worldly pleasures does not mean distancing oneself from people or isolation, since that would be foreign to Christ's spirit. On the contrary, that life choice requires a commitment to service. But service is not only a question of giving food and drink to the poor. Prayer, studies, intellectual production, and teaching are also expressions of service.

The churches and homosexuality

A moral problem being raised in the churches, in a more and more open manner, is that of homosexuality. Here too, obviously, we are dealing with a problem that has always existed but is coming to light today. Homosexuals are demanding that their rights be recognized by society and by the churches. At the European Ecumenical Assembly in Graz, in the agora, *the pavilion of stands for different ecumenical groups and movements, there was also a stand for homosexual Christians.*

What is your position concerning homosexuality?

I think that you are right to say that this phenomenon has always existed. Today, it is the socialization of that phenomenon that is in question. Our permissive society, which understands its freedom as a lifestyle without any limits or criteria, and the preeminent place that the media accords to everything having to do with unregulated sexuality, have made it such that this problem has taken on great proportions.

While taking into account each particular case and having a pastoral concern for the people involved, the Church cannot accept that a reality manifestly opposed to the teaching of the Bible be considered normal. That would bring in to question our fidelity to God's Word. Even though it has always existed in the Church as well as in society, homosexuality has always been considered a deviation. Why should we now accept this phenomenon as normal? That extremely permissive attitude leads to a moral relativism in which you can no longer distinguish good from evil.

You know, however, that today, the laws of certain countries allow homosexuals to marry each other and to form a family that has the same rights as a heterosexual family in matters such as inheritance, the adoption of children, etc.

I cannot approve of that. I am convinced that no good for society will result from it. On the contrary, we will see more serious and difficult problems arise. Some countries have laws that are completely outside the scope of Christian morality. I think that that is very dangerous because if you touch these basic moral principles, we fall into total moral anarchy. Both man and society need "constitutive norms," as Father Yves Congar would often say.

The Church and morality

I would like to extend our conversation on morality to the question of life. Pope John Paul II, throughout his pontificate, has emphasized the value of human life and institutions' duty to defend it from the first moment of conception until the last breath. That implies a moral condemnation of abortion, despite most countries' laws, of suicide, of euthanasia…

Without entering into the complicated details of each specific case, what is your Church's position concerning the defense of human life?

Human life was not created by man; thus it is not his property. Life is a gift from God. That means that we must be accountable for this gift to Him who gave it to us. We are neither the masters of our life nor the masters of our bodies, and we cannot do with them as we please, according to our whims. Human life has a sacred character that must be respected.

In our Church, we have not formulated particular moral rules concerning this matter; we have not made specific decisions or made official declarations for each moral problem. But our Church exhorts its followers to respect the sacred character of life from its beginning and not to resort to abortion, which ends life.

Some Catholics deplore the fact that their Church has a morality that is too "narrow" where sexuality is concerned. They find the fact that the Church gives norms not only on abortion but on genetic manipulation and contraception untimely.

Eastern churches do not have a moral, sexual doctrine as precise as the Catholic Church's...

In our Eastern tradition, we have always judged that the Church's task is to form the Christian conscience of the people by giving them only the principal directives for behavior in a life that conforms to God's will. But we do not interfere with the details, which are often relative and scientifically debatable. We do not go into the intimate domain of each person's life.

I think that it is our duty to respect the freedom that God has given everyone, and at the same time, to find believers in the execution of that freedom, to feed their awareness, and help them grow. However, the Church must not make rules that sweep aside the people's conscience. It is not a question of a moral liberalism or relativism, but of allowing each person the ability to exercise his own conscience.

This reflects the confidence that the Church has in its followers. Since they have received the grace of God and a Christian education, the Church considers them ready to distinguish good from evil.

CHAPTER VIII

The Mystery of the
Church in the World

The Church in society

*The Church is the mystical body of Christ; as such, it transcends
time and space. On the other hand, it is as the mystical body of
Christ on Earth that it must continue its work here and now.
That consists of a responsible commitment to society, a stand
with respect to the problems of our world: poverty, social injustice, discrimination, racism, but also ecology, technological progress, etc. It is the tricky problem of "the Church and politics,"
in the fullest sense that the latter term has in Greek, which I
would like to discuss today.*

*For some people, a church that is involved with too many
"things of the world" is a secular, lay church. On the other hand,
not to be engaged in social issues would be, for the Church, to
betray Christ's call to be the light of the world, and the Church
would be no more than a sort of spiritual Rotary club.*

The Church can never remain indifferent to the problems
of the world. The world is God's creation, and so for the
Christian, it is a sacred reality. Jesus said that the apostles,
like Himself, were not of this world; but He never said that

they must be outside of this world. On the contrary, He
begged the Father to keep them in this world (Jn 17:15). It
is a question of seeing whether that presence in the world,
which is always a service, is an *identification* with the
world, or an *opposition* to it…. Where there is injustice, op-
pression, discrimination, the Church must not remove
itself from the situation by claiming that it is an affair of
the State that does not concern the spirit. The Church cannot ignore any man's suffering or the injustice perpetrated
against any individual, group or nation.

It is an entirely different thing to say that the Church's
positions must not be dictated by political interests, that is
to say, by a narrow approach, by the advantages of this or
that party, but by the concern for all men. Similarly, the
Church must not identify its mission on Earth with a specific solution to these problems, linked to a particular ideology or system. Thus, if the Church cannot courageously
and firmly say what truth and justice require it to—as in-
convenient or disconcerting as it may be—that means that
it has become just another political institution.

In your book In Search of Spiritual Life, *you wrote:*

> *If you are indifferent to human necessities, how can you
> claim to be Christians? When He saw a blind man, Christ
> did not talk to him about light, but He opened his eyes,
> when He saw a deaf man, He did not talk to him about the
> beauty of sounds, He opened his ears… Christ became in-
> carnate, which means that He identified himself with
> human beings.*

Does that mean that the Church has a duty to feed the hungry, provide shelter for the homeless, etc.? Or, at the very least, to be an advocate for the marginalized and give moral directions condemning all social injustice?

I think that the Church must not only condemn with words, through directives, the evils of society; it must also commit itself on a personal level and participate in the reduction and elimination of these evils. The Church has offered certain social services of which it is very proud for centuries. I remember that a Muslim political leader from a country of the Near East said, "I cannot accept the teachings of Christ or your faith, such as the Trinity; but I bow before those sisters" — he was referring to Catholic nuns — "who left their comfortable countries to serve and take care of our sick, handicapped, orphans, elderly...." That is how the testimony of the Church becomes credible, by not limiting itself to only preaching but by engaging in concrete service.

It is obvious that we cannot heal all the wounds in this world, but we must do all that we can, the maximum.

Church and state

Church and State: a balance that has never been easy. Armenia is a Christian country. Does it also wish to be a Christian state? People talk a lot today about the notions of a secular state and a denominational state. Most Western Christians are for a secular state. In the East, where orthodox churches are national churches, the issue is situated differently. However, many orthodox theologians support the idea of a secular state.

Will the Armenia of the future be a denominational state? A secular state? A theocracy?

A return to obsolete institutions, like a theocracy, does not seem possible to me. Today, with the proclamation of independence, the idea of a secular state is asserting itself more and more in our country. I think that the state has some distinct functions that we must recognize and that are very different from the Church's goals. Jesus Himself made that distinction by exhorting his followers to give to Caesar what is Caesar's and to God what is God's...

However, that distinction does not imply a total reciprocal ignorance. Today, the Armenian state gives enough importance to the Church as a spiritual and moral force that can contribute to the blossoming of the nation. The state needs faith and the Church. Among other things, this has been proven to us by the experience of the last seventy years, the experience of an attempt to eliminate faith.

Moreover, we must not forget that historically the Christian faith in Armenia has been expressed in the nation's life through the Armenian Apostolic Church. In the seventeen centuries that followed the adoption of Christianity, the process of the *enculturation* of the faith has been carried out in the context of the Armenian Church; so the Church became and remains the center of the spiritual life of the people of Armenia. It is in this sense that the Armenian Church is not the religion of the state, but the national religion of Armenia.

In each country, there must be an agreement between the State and the churches. In countries where a Church is a clear major-

ity and has its roots deep in the history of the nation, it is
natural that there would be a preferential agreement between the
State and that church.

Recently in Russia, the promulgation of a law on religious
organizations, which seemed to strongly restrict denominations
other than the Orthodox Church, created a great deal of contro-
versy. In the new Armenia, .will there be a place for other
denominations?

Religious freedom is recognized and guaranteed by the
Constitution of our state. Each citizen can choose the religious denomination that he wants.

The Armenian Apostolic Church has always been integrated into the life of the nation in an existential way; this
is a historical fact that cannot be ignored. The Armenian
Catholic Church and the Armenian Evangelical Church,
which were present in Armenia well before and even
during (in the case of the latter) the Soviet regime, are recognized by the state. We work in cooperation with them.

An entirely different aspect of that question is the avalanche of sects. There, the freedoms of religion and conscience exist, but the issue is to see how these sects use
them. Very often, the economic and psychological means
used by these organizations to gain followers are, at the
very least, questionable. When someone is looking to
"buy" people's faith, or to give financial help to the poor in
return for loyalty to a sect or a church, that is a dishonest
exploitation of religious freedom. That is something that
has to do with aggressive proselytism, denounced by all of
the churches involved in ecumenism.

Our Catholic and Evangelical brothers are welcome in
our country because they take care of their own; but if they

fall back into the type of action that the missionaries of the nineteenth century practiced, that, to me, would be a betrayal of everything that these decades of ecumenism have given us. Ecumenism began through mutual respect. Today, the Christian mission cannot identify itself with proselytism, but must promote faith in each country according to the traditions that have always characterized Christianity over the centuries. Competition and proselytism only distance people from the churches; today we need cooperation among Christians. Without that cooperation, we will see a situation of spiritual confusion created in a people awakening to the Christian faith.

The Church and social justice

One of the problems that the republics of the ex-Soviet Union must face is the distribution of wealth. The savage capitalism that has taken hold in the wake of the end of Communism seems to be leading these countries toward a South American social model of a social gap between the small minority of the wealthy and the rest of the population.

What can the Church do in this situation?

The situations of the countries of the former Soviet Union are, in reality, rather different from one another. Here in Armenia, many of our social problems are still the result of the former system or of its breakdown. We have few natural resources, and our country must face the blockage situation created by the Nagorno-Karabagh conflict and exacerbated by the fact that, having no access to the sea, our relationships with other countries have become very difficult.

The danger of a rather radical economic difference between the rich and the poor also exists in Armenia. We are already seeing the signs of a socio-economic inequality that is preventing the general progress of the people. I fear that they may be the signs of an ill-conceived capitalism. In this situation, the Church must certainly give moral instruction and commit itself to helping the disadvantaged. But that commitment cannot be only moral or verbal. That is why we have organized social services in the Church for unemployed people; we have modest funds from which we lend small sums of money to people who work on some job or other. The goal is for everyone to be able to earn a living through their own work. Aside from that, we have volunteers in state orphanages and hospitals, which, unfortunately, are often in deplorable condition. We are also in the process of planning other projects to help the handicapped, the elderly, etc. These projects are supported for the most part by Armenians from the diaspora; we have a lot of hope in the ecumenical institutions.

What is important in this area is that the government and the entrepreneurs from the private sector adopt policies that target local development. Our political independence must be nourished by an economy of self-reliance that can give everyone the possibility of elevating their level of life and their human dignity.

At the international level, the same problem of the distribution of wealth is happening in a dramatic way, in which we can see a new division of the world in two: the North and the South. Today, the world's wealth is concentrated in the Western half of

Europe (the other half is slowly getting back on its feet), in North America, Australia, some countries in Asia and a few countries in Africa. The rest of the world, including some heavily populated countries (like India, Indonesia, Pakistan, Brazil), is under-nourished and under-developed.

This is the great social challenge of the coming century. Do you think that the churches have something to say about it?

Yes. The unity of humanity must always be the focus of the Church's concerns. When faced with inequality, injustice, or the polarizations that have undermined the unity of our world, as was the case in the past with the division of East-West and now of North-South, the Church cannot *not* raise its voice and offer its hands. How is it possible that on our planet at the end of the twentieth century, there are still thousands of people dying in under-fed countries, and that other countries are what we call "over-developed"? How is it possible that the countries in which there is great affluence and wealth do not succeed in sharing with those who are immediately in need?

In our times, we have talked a lot about man's rights, but not enough about man's duties, as Solzhenitsyn noted a long time ago. Development without a sense of duty towards the poor, the needy, is not human. I think that in its preaching of the truth, the Church must make itself the bearer of the idea of economic equality for humanity.

We must rediscover the *diaconate*, because the Church has been called to fully express Christ's ministry, which did not only consist in preaching and prayer, but was also a service for the concrete human needs of the people. On that matter, it is significant that the epithet of the "*good shepherd*," which Christ applies to Himself in Saint John's

Gospel (Jn 10:11-14), is translated in our Armenian version as the *"courageous shepherd."* That truly captures the attitude of active engagement of that shepherd, who is not afraid of the wolf and ready to give his life for his sheep, to find them when they are lost, to care for them.

Christian communism?

You were talking about economic equality… You know that for more than a century, that idea was proclaimed and spread by Communism. As a political system, Communism seems to have been removed from the world scene. Do you think that in the century to come, it will be the Church's job to pursue the idea of the economic equality of men?

First of all, I want to affirm that the equality of which the Communists spoke was far from actually existing in Communist countries…

What I call *equality* should not be understood as an economic leveling, since there will always be people who work more than others or who are more talented or smarter than others, and consequently, there will be different economic levels. It is more a question of free and spontaneous sharing, but which can be organized. The equality of the world in the Christian sense is the communion of nations, races, and cultures, which corresponds to God's design for humanity. For me, the question of equality is a question of justice.

Communism, which in its theories denied the very idea of God, sought to attain the equality of men without God. However, as

*paradoxical as it may seem, the roots of the communist ideal of
equality are found in Christianity. The Acts of the Apostles show
us the practice of common ownership of the community goods in
Jerusalem, where believers shared everything that they owned
and each person received money, according to his needs, from the
community...*

*Do you think that a kind of "Christian communism" could
exist?*

The expression "communism" is so charged with negative
connotations that I cannot associate those two words...

The case of which you are speaking, that of the first
Church of Jerusalem, concerned a small community, which
was not yet structured and where the mutual love shared
by everyone was a driving force. With the diffusion of
Christianity, the concrete form of this sharing of goods
changed. Today, unfortunately, we do not always have
that spiritual environment of a living community with the
sharing of goods in the Church. But although the concrete
forms of that practice are different, the spirit must be the
same as that of the first Christians: we must come to a
situation of sharing freely with the needy.

I think that in our modern society, so technically
organized, we must find much more efficient means to
realize the sharing of goods. Sharing is the source of happiness, precisely that happiness that is lacking in our civilization. We have become individualists, and the Church
must react against that tendency by teaching how to share,
primarily through its example.

It is a duty of my conscience for me to say how happy I
am to see that today, thanks to the World Council of
Churches as well as certain charitable organizations of the

Catholic Church (like Caritas International and others), the sharing of goods is picking up speed and reaching a wider range in ecumenical relations.

Progress and new problems

Scientific and technical progress poses new moral questions for the churches. That is the case for bioethics. Recently, Scottish biologists, by manipulating the genetic code of a cell, created a "clone" – an identical copy – of a sheep.

Science today is capable of "building" plants and animals in laboratories. Maybe in the future, it will even be able to plan and actualize human beings "on command," with very specific characteristics: eye and hair color, maybe also personality, tastes...

What do you think of that?

I am completely against that type of manipulation in matters concerning human life. The gift of God that is life is the greatest mystery of creation. To make man the product of an industry or a laboratory would be to ridicule the sacred sense of human life. I do not know whether science, through cloning or other means, will succeed one day in "fabricating" men, but in my opinion, we must renounce these experiments. I think that legislation should impose limits on this research.

Here, it is the meaning of human life that is at stake; if we can produce and create it in this manner, man, the subject, becomes an object. The freedom to conduct research cannot go against the freedom given to a human being with the free gift of life, whose source is God. In my understanding, genetic manipulation is something that manifestly goes against God's will. If it is applied to man, then tomorrow we will find ourselves facing unimaginable and insurmountable problems.

The total lack of moral principles comes from the fact that man sees his life as his property, his private affair.

An urgent problem in our world is that of the environment. It has been calculated that in the coming decades, if atmospheric pollution continues at its current pace, then the global temperature will rise by a few degrees, which would cause the ice of the Antarctic to melt. It follows that many coasts will be submerged, entire countries will disappear from the map of the world...

But, in addition to atmospheric pollution, we must also consider the continual cutting of trees (for example, the destruction of the Amazon forest), the exhaustion of soil, the desertification of vast regions of the planet (like the expansion of the Sahara desert), the extermination of thousands of species of animals, water pollution, the poisoning of bodies of water because of the use of agricultural chemicals...

Overall, today man is at a point where he runs the risk of destroying the planet. What can the Church say when faced with this kind of collective suicide?

First, I would like to react to your question by saying that the picture that you just painted seems too somber to me, even a bit apocalyptic! I understand well that the elements of that illustration came to you from scientific data; but God, who is the Creator and master of the universe, can always save His creation. I do not know why, but I am confident that the future will not be as somber as some environmentalists claim.

But let's get to your question. The Church must show in a clear and strong manner its concern for God's creation. For believers, nature is, above all else, God's creation, of which we are a part. The manipulation of that creation, the violence that people do to nature, is also manifestly against God's will. Our progress leads us to repeat Adam's sin: to believe that we are gods, the bosses and masters of everything.

God entrusted the world He created to man, who through science and technology may *use* natural resources, but he must not *waste* them. The problem of the environment is truly one of the most serious problems of our time. I am delighted that certain states today have adopted an ecological policy that is more determined to limit pollution. We should not forget that it remains difficult for poor countries. Since the threat is serious, I think that our efforts to stop pollution and all of man's violence against nature should be multiplied.

At the same time, as I said, faced with this ecological catastrophe, I personally am keeping an inner feeling of tranquility because I am sure that the world will remain in God's hands. And God, in His love, will make us aware of our sin against Creation and nature.

"I have sinned against nature..."

You are talking about sin: maybe today, there are new sins, the "anti-ecological" sins. Polluting rivers, setting fire to woods, and maybe even throwing a cigarette butt onto the street... Are these sins?

I think so. That sin is the lack of responsibility with respect
to nature, the refusal to respond with good to the good
that God gave us through His gift of creation. Everything
that is harmful to nature, to the sea, to the atmosphere,
goes against God's work. In the list of sins found in our
liturgical formulation of confession, maybe we could add:
"I have sinned against nature, the source of our food and
the place of our happiness."

*Recently, the churches have almost "discovered" ecology. Since
the European Ecumenical Assembly in Basel in 1989, one of the
goals of the ecumenical movement seems to be the protection of
Creation. The very expression "ecumenical," in its principal
meaning in the Greek word* oïkoumene, *signifies "all of the
inhabited Earth," all of humanity — as if to tell us that the continuation of life on this planet depends upon a common effort
that all Christians must make together.*

I agree and I like your observation. Ecology, the commitment to the defense of Creation, is also an area for ecumenism because from that perspective, I cannot imagine that
there would be any divergences among the churches. On
the contrary, that common solicitude might even reduce
the acuity of dogmatic differences! The churches must
forcefully reaffirm the duty of Christians to defend nature
because God has entrusted Creation to man so that he can
be its guardian, and not so that he can manipulate it as he
pleases.

Fortunately, the stand that the churches have taken has
already taken hold. For example, the World Council of
Churches has conducted in-depth studies on the signifi-

cance of creation in relation to justice and peace; there have been numerous international consultations on that subject.

Pope John Paul II, in his encyclicals, has often tackled that problem, particularly in his encyclical *Veritatis splendor* on human life.

When Ecumenical Patriarch Bartholomew I was visiting Etchmiadzin, we talked at length about that, and I followed very attentively the work of the conferences dedicated to ecology, which he organized in Constantinople and on Halki with the participation of representatives of several churches and Prince Philip, the Duke of Edinburgh. The last of these conferences, which took place on a boat, was dedicated to the problem of the pollution of the Black Sea region. I was represented there by an Armenian bishop.

So there are concrete indications that the churches and the ecumenical world are seriously committed to the protection of nature. I think that in the future, this ecumenical action will be reinforced and will give us more tangible results.

The Church and culture

In Armenia's history, the Church has played a fundamental cultural role. Armenian culture is filled with the Christian faith. Several figures in your cultural history were ecclesiastics, beginning with Saint Mesrob Mashtots, who invented your alphabet, and Catholicos Sahak, who with his translation of the Bible, liturgical and patristic texts inaugurated your Golden Age of literature, and up to the return of Armenian culture and literature in the eighteenth century with the work of the Armenian Benedictine Catholic Mekhitar.

What is the Armenian Church's relationship with the Armenian national culture today?

Our era is very different from the fifth century as well as from the eighteenth century—and those centuries are very different from each other. The role of Abbot Mekhitar and the Mekhitarist fathers in the awakening of the Armenian culture is very significant, but you cannot attribute all the cultural rebirth of that time to a single Mekhitarist movement. In the eighteenth century there were other culturally active monasteries in Armenia and especially in Constantinople. Besides, although there was a return of Armenian literature and culture in the eighteenth century, the true rebirth was in the nineteenth century, with the contact we had with Western culture.

With the nineteenth century, lay people participated more in cultural life. This did not mean that the Church was not contributing culturally, as the monasteries remained important cultural centers in Armenia, in Tblisi, in Constantinople, and wherever our people were living, often in spite of historical turmoil.

Today, after the fall of the Soviet Union, the Church here in Armenia wants to commit, on a personal level, to the development of the culture. I am happy to say that there is a continual and growing effort to reunite our culture to spiritual values.

I think that today, secularism has begun to dominate in Armenia as well. The applied sciences, technology, and industry have engendered a kind of materialism, which has become the principal psychology of our consumer society. The culture is now deprived of its traditional values; the

Church's contribution to culture must thus help in the rediscovery of spiritual values.

People talk a lot about *enculturation*: the Christian faith must be expressed within the parameters of each particular culture. But enculturation is a path with two meanings, a question of interpretation, of synthesis and meeting between the Good News and human culture. The Church cannot ignore or neglect the great discoveries of the new scientific culture, which, among other things, are doing a great service for God's creatures. The issue is to understand how to instill a sense of the spiritual value of man in that culture so that man does not become a machine, which would impoverish humanity. On the contrary, the common goal of religion, science and culture is the blossoming of man in his integrity, including his material, spiritual, intellectual and moral aspects.

Enculturation and the consumer society

You are talking about enculturation and secularism. A good example of enculturation is without doubt the essential work of the Fathers of the Church in the first centuries of the Christian Era: they knew how to express the Christian message in the categories of Greek philosophical thought. First, the Church confronted secular thought, in the time of the Fathers, and arrived at a new synthesis: nothing has changed in the Christian doctrine, but it has found a new expression.

Several times in its history, the Church has confronted secular philosophies (for example, Humanism at the end of the Middle Ages, or Rationalism in the Age of Enlightenment) and knew how to surpass these crises in different ways. Since every culture evolves over time, enculturation is not only welcoming the cultural values of a people, but also those of a century, of an era.

The last cultural challenge that your Church has known came from Communism and its atheist ideology. Now a challenge is presented to you by the society of consumption, with secularism. How will you respond to it?

There are two things that seem important to me for the new post-Soviet period. The first is the rediscovery of what we had before Communism from our cultural Christian roots. Second, we must keep our relations with other cultures; we cannot shut ourselves off in isolation. Our period demands dialogue between civilizations.

But that is not an easy thing. We just came out of the state of forced isolation in which we found ourselves under the Soviet regime. In reaction to this, we seek out everything that was once forbidden, to such a point that we have lost our sense of judgment, the ability to choose. Before the avalanche of Western influences, people were unable to distinguish good grain from straw. In the great moral confusion of this transitional period, I think that the Church, the State, the diaspora and all our non-Armenian friends who wish to help us must make an effort to bring these true values to light.

The lifestyle that we call "Western," which is now coming to former socialist countries, is in reality the pseudo-culture of the society of consumption, which makes all cultures uniform and flat. In the West, since this phenomenon has grown slowly, people have had the time to develop "antibodies," an immunizing tool against this epidemic, while here, people often cannot defend

themselves. Faced with this phenomenon, people are seeing a re-
awakening of nationalism; to defend their identity, they shut
themselves into their own culture.

You talk, by contrast, about opening up and about an inter-
cultural dialogue. How do we go beyond extremist nationalism?

First, we must see the positive side of nationalism: the
sense of national identity. Human beings are not born
from nothing. They have inherited the values from their
history. I remember an expression of Edouard Baladur, the
former prime minister of France, who said that "France is
not Nature's creation; it is *history's* creation."

How true that is for Armenia! For us Armenians, the
sense of national belonging has become very dear, not only
because of Communism, but also because of the events
that we have survived throughout history and that threat-
ened our national identity.

But that sense of identity cannot be an exclusivism.
Nationalism for me has nothing to do with the fanaticism
that makes one's own nation an idol. In my understanding, nationalism is the awareness of belonging to a specific
identity. Affirming one's identity does not imply cutting
off communication with others. On the contrary, that
identity needs to be in relation with others to avoid suffo-
cating.

I think that at this time in Armenia, we are witnessing
a national awakening and a flourishing of exchanges with
the rest of the world. The harmonious combination of
these two movements is very promising.

Jesus Christ, the first secularist

I would like to return to the concept of secularism. We have spoken about the fact that in the course of the history, the Church has been able to question itself while also going through crises.

The secularism that all churches complain about, because it is manifested as a negation of the Church and what is holy, may not be entirely negative. It is a new challenge for Christianity... Couldn't secularism help us to rediscover spiritual values in a purified form, without the clericalism of the past?

I think that before anything else, it is necessary to ask ourselves what we call material. We must go beyond the old dichotomy of material-spiritual, which remains prevalent. We Christians must see the work of God in the material. Someone said, "Culture is the spirit's pressure on the material."

Second, in the complex phenomenon of secularism, we must distinguish between what can be positive and useful and what is exasperation, the negation of transcendence. If secularism signifies recognizing the value of all aspects of human life, temporal activities as well as the sacred, then Jesus Christ was one of the precursors of secularism. In His doctrine, we find no opposition between the profane and the sacred, as all aspects of human life were important to Him. He shows this through His participation in the wedding at Cana, through the fact that He shared His people's lives in every way...

Another thing is the degeneracy of that tendency to affirm the dignity of earthly realities, the exasperating tendency that excludes the presence of God in human life. Some of our contemporaries say, "We don't need God because we have achieved such progress that we cannot tolerate being dependent upon a Supreme Being." I believe that such an exacerbated secularism has not provided any happiness to humanity. But that negative assessment is a very healthy challenge for the Church, a challenge that we must take seriously.

CHAPTER IX

Ecumenism

The good thief and dogmatism

*"Outside of the Church, no salvation," said the Catholic cate-
chisms from the beginning of the twentieth century. The same
thing, "Outside of our church, there is no salvation," is repeated
today by many orthodox followers. Does eternal salvation depend
on the church one belongs to?*

I think that this is a question of our conception of salvation. If we call our Lord Jesus Christ *"Savior,"* that means
that it is *He* who gives salvation freely to those whom He
deems worthy. On this matter, we must remember the
good thief, crucified beside Jesus, when he recognized that
the pain that Jesus suffered was unjust and said to Him,
"Remember me when you enter your Kingdom." He
recognized a divine presence in the person of Christ; and
Jesus turned to him and said, "Today you will be with me
in the Kingdom of Heaven." That tells us that the act of
salvation is a divine act, that He who grants salvation is
the Savior Himself.

However, the expression "outside of the Church, no salvation" *does* have a meaning, and a very important one, especially if you are not referring in a narrow or exclusivist sense to this or that denominational church, but to the Church as the Mystical Body of Christ. It means that the so-to-speak "ordinary" path to salvation is the Church, created by Christ for the world's salvation. But God transcends what He created. He, who is all-powerful and infinite love, remains above the Church and does not limit salvation exclusively to the domain of the Church. Thus, salvation is the vocation, the mission and the function of the Church, but it is not its sole prerogative. We must not limit God or substitute ourselves for Him to establish the criteria and the conditions for salvation. The grace of God is overabundant and it can also affect people outside of institutional churches.

You are familiar with the words of Saint Paul: "If with your mouth you affirm before all that Jesus is the Lord, and if you believe in your heart that God has raised Him from death, then you will be saved" (Rom 10:9). To believe that God has brought back Jesus from the dead implies one's faith in the Resurrection. That is one of the criteria for salvation that is linked to faith, but not to this or that Christian tradition, since the profession of faith that Jesus is the Lord and that God raised Him is common to all Christians.

Without faith in the Resurrection, there would be no Church; the Church was born from that faith, and it was its first home. But faith also needs the Church because, as I have said several times, the Christian faith is not an abstract doctrine, but a life which must be embodied in a community, the Church. That is why, in this sense, it is very right to say, "Outside of the Church, no salvation."

One could say that professing one's faith in the Resurrection is what characterizes the good thief, whom you just cited, since he recognized that Jesus was going to enter His Kingdom.

Of course. It may have only been an intuitive faith, but he certainly felt that that man crucified next to him was the Savior.

I remember the words of an Armenian theologian from the fifth century who said that "each soldier who gave his life for his faith was a Church unto himself."

What do you think of the position of Christians who are convinced that there is no salvation outside of the ecclesiastical tradition to which they belong?

Those people only have to wait for the Second Coming...

What I mean is that I do not approve of such a narrow dogmatism, which seems to me rather egocentric. I think that each one of us can indicate or propose to others the path to salvation of our own institutional Church, but we cannot deny that God can touch a person where He wants, when He wants. That is a spiritual arrogance and would mean that we are making ourselves the masters and judges of our neighbors, and not serving them. It would be like taking the place of the supreme Judge. I have never approved of the attitude of people who are sure that they will be saved. God is the Lord of salvation, and that absolute truth must not be questioned.

Ecumenism and the ecumenical movement

The word ecumenism may need to be more precisely defined today. For some people, it has taken on a negative connotation, and others prefer not to use it. There is formal ecumenism, consisting of diplomatic relations between the churches, the ecumenism of symbolic gestures, the ecumenism of theological dialogue...

What is ecumenism for you?

For me, ecumenism is a deeply spiritual reality; it is a dimension of the very essence of our Christian faith. We must refer to Chapter Seventeen of Saint John's Gospel, in which the will of our Lord Jesus Christ clearly shows us: "Father, let all be one... Let them be one... so that the world may believe that you have sent me." This is not just a desire like any other; the credibility of the Christian faith is inextricably linked to that quality of ecclesiastical existence, to the fact that we show in our lives the unity given to us by Christ, the unity that is the very life of the Holy Trinity.

If by the word *ecumenism*, we are designating the constant quest to manifest that part of God's will, then that is the duty of all the churches and every Christian. In this way, ecumenism is a part of the very definition of the Church because unity is at the heart of the Church's work and existence.

Then, we must also distinguish between *ecumenism* as such and the *ecumenical movement*, which gives itself this or that concrete objective. In the ecumenical movement (I am referring to the World Council of Churches, but also to other organizations) we try by all means to make the quest for unity the central theme of our theological reflection and of our common actions.

Certainly, some events and expressions of the ecumenical movement have not always been faithful to the authentic spirit of ecumenism. But that is similar to the question of sainthood, which is the vocation of every Christian—you never reach the summit, and you might experience failure. Similarly, on the ecumenical path, there are also steps backward, but they do not threaten the essence of the process. On the path toward complete unity of the churches, there are obstacles. But we must never be discouraged; we must always remain engaged in dialogue, in communication, in spite of all difficulties. Our movement toward unity is a duty, an imperative that we have received from our Lord, and in spite of our human fragility, all of our weaknesses and shortcomings, we must never renounce it.

Unity and love

You are talking about unity. In studying your biography, one could say that unity is the driving force behind your life. As a bishop and Catholicos, you have committed yourself to uniting the two Catholicossates by putting an end to the distance that has existed between the two for so long. In the conflict that devastated Lebanon, your second homeland, you called several times for the diverse communities to unite. As an activist at the forefront of the ecumenical movement, you are pursuing the

unity of the churches.   As Catholicos of All Armenians, you
symbolize the unity of the diaspora with the homeland.
   What is unity to you?

Unity is an attitude of the spirit, a force that has three
poles: unity is a relation to God, composed of fidelity; it is
a relation to others, those who profess the same Christ; and
thirdly, it is fidelity to oneself. Love, before being a person's feeling of goodness towards another, is belonging to
the same source, which is God. It is a question of being. If
God is love, as the Scripture says, then *we* must *also* be
love, a reflection of God's essence.   And—let us never
forget!—love does not know divisions; it is the *antidote* to
division.

   That is why I think that if we put this dimension of
universal love towards God, others and oneself above any
other dogmatic, intellectual, or cultural consideration, then
any kind of dialogue is possible. What is important in ecumenism is not really the process of exchanging theological
reflections, but the manifestation of this love. When I say
that, I do not want to minimize the importance of theological conversations, inter-ecclesiastical meetings or common
actions. But if all of these elements, which are what ecumenical action consists of, are not put in motion, nourished
and guided by love, then they will never be fruitful.

   I ask myself the fundamental question: what kind of
force did Jesus use to win over His disciples? Even before
intriguing them intellectually with His doctrine, He en-
chanted them with the force of His love, which emanated
from His person. The first Christians, the martyrs, spread
the faith through love.

Saint John teaches us that God is love; God, One in three Per-
sons, is unity. It is love, God's essence, which makes His unity
something other than monolithic. This should give us a methodo-
logical indication for the quest for unity, the goal of ecumenism.

The devil – "the accuser, the slanderer," which is what the
Greek word diabolos *means – is primarily the agent who*
"divides," who breaks that which is united, since this is the ety-
mological meaning of the word diaballein, *from which the word*
is derived...

Your remark is very fair; the lack of light we are experiencing, the darkness, the lack of love and unity, is an effect of
the work of the "separator." Human history is full of mistakes. Those who want to engage in ecumenism must look
at history and distinguish when and how our fathers have
been without that love because they did not have unity.
But after acknowledging these mistakes, we must move on
to reparation. To acknowledge, to historically explain this
separation must necessarily lead to the reconstitution of
what was lost or destroyed: unity in love. The evil of
separation must be reduced, vanquished and eliminated
by love, which is the source of all good and all happiness.

Looking at what unites us

According to John Paul II's expression, you are "one of the pio-
neers of ecumenism." How did your commitment to ecumenism
begin?

I have been involved in the ecumenical movement since
the first days of my diaconate, when I was still a student. I
followed the nascent spirituality of ecumenism, which

emanated, for example, from Abbot Couturier of Lyon. My first ecumenical gathering was a meeting with the directors of Christian university movements in the Near East in 1955. I remember the great figure of ecumenism William Visser't Hooft, one of the founders of the World Council of Churches, whom I consider a spiritual father. With a prophetic spirit, he predicted a renaissance of the ancient Eastern churches, and with all his means encouraged the young priests and lay theologians of the Orthodox churches. In his memoirs, which were published in English, he refers to that very gathering of young people in Beirut: "The day of rebirth was being prepared in the oldest churches of Christianity." Then I met Father Florovsky, Professor Alivisatos, Father Congar, Cardinals Bea and Willebrands.... Those eminent figures of true ecumenism strongly influenced my thought, my ministry and my life.

Since you are asking me about my ecumenical beginnings, I will tell you the story of an event that I have never written about, which influenced my commitment to the unity of churches. In 1961, His Grace Bishop Willebrands, not yet a cardinal, came to Antelias to speak with the Catholicos at that time, the great Catholicos Zareh I, who was endowed with an exemplary ecumenical spirit. Very delicately, he asked him the following question, more or less in these terms: In case the Pope convenes a Council in the Vatican and invites a representative from our church, would we be ready to participate? And our Catholicos replied immediately: "But does a man who invites his brother doubt that he will accept?" That was the feeling of unity that he had. Then he added: "If we synthesize all of the teachings of the Gospel in one hundred points, don't you think that we would agree on ninety-nine of them? However, unfortunately, we often only talk about the one point on which our opinions separate us, forgetting how much we have in common...." He pointed to the wall before him: "If there were a little black spot on this white wall, we would forget the whiteness of the wall to talk about the little stain..."

What I learned is that today, we must, on the contrary, look at what unites us. For me, this is the true strategy—if I can speak so—of ecumenism, which must allow us to move into the third millennium.

But how can you do this concretely – where do you begin?

I have said elsewhere that the Church is one in Christ's conception, and that *in spite* of our divisions, that unity remains. The unity of Christians *exists*, and we do not need to go look for it outside because it is already in us; we all have the same Gospel, and we all follow Christ. Now, the Church's spiritual, mystical unity, which we all profess in the Creed, must be expressed, manifested on the outside in the lives of our different churches. This is the goal of ecumenism.

For that, common prayer is the most important element. Common dialogue, study and action are the authentic content of the ecumenical movement. What is fundamental is not the meetings of heads of churches, hierarchs or the innumerable consultations, commissions, conferences, etc., but the opening up of one to the other. That is exactly what Father Congar says with the final words of his spiritual testament. I remember him well.

When I was an observer at the Second Vatican Council, he often said to me that ecumenism for him was an inherent vocation of the Church, the authentic manifestation of our Christian faith.

The Orthodox churches and ecumenism

You made a distinction between ecumenism as a movement towards unity that must be made by all of the churches and by all Christians, and the concrete actualizations of the ecumenical movement, which can be more or less fair or limited. Unfortunately, the fact that that distinction is not clear creates misunderstandings.

Recently, in Orthodox churches, people have observed a sort of hesitation with respect to the World Council of Churches and ecumenism in general. Some orthodox followers see a kind of sin there. In Moscow, in the kiosks of several churches, you can buy a brochure entitled "Ecumenism, a path that leads to perdition." At the root of the Georgian churches departure from the World Council of Churches was a letter addressed to Patriarch Ilya II by a group of monks in which ecumenism is defined as the "heresy of heresies." How do you explain that mistrust, or maybe even fear, of certain Orthodox milieu regarding ecumenism?

First, I would like to make people see that that negative approach to ecumenism does not only involve the family of Orthodox churches. I have seen movements reacting to ecumenism in the heart of the Roman Catholic Church. I myself have heard a Catholic bishop in the United States say that where ecumenism is concerned, "it is necessary to undo what Vatican II has done." Also, you are familiar with Archbishop Lefebvre's movement. Similarly, in some sectors of Protestantism, there are some radical evangelical movements that reject ecumenism. So this reaction to ecumenism exists a little in all churches.

As for the Orthodox churches, first of all I see two reasons for this mistrust. First, in some churches that are members of the World Council of Churches, you see some extremely liberal tendencies and movements in the domains of theology and ethics that are manifestly against our tradition and that, in our opinion, contradict Christ's teachings. Orthodox followers cannot compromise the integrity of the orthodoxy of the Christian faith, which they have kept at the price of bloodshed.

Second, I think that within each Orthodox church, we do not work enough to communicate the authentic spirit and the true nature of ecumenism to our followers. I mean that the results of the ecumenical movement have not been adequately preached, spread, and interpreted in our churches, so that they become a part of the people's lives, the lives of all of our followers. Ecumenism is not a line of action taken somewhere in Geneva, New York, Canterbury or Rome, but within every church.

So now, in the eyes of some Orthodox followers, ecumenism looks like a sort of enclave of Protestantism in the heart of Orthodoxy. Imagine that a member of the Russian Church who was very involved in the ecumenical movement said to me one day in Geneva that his followers confused the word "ecumenism" with "communism".... There is still much ignorance to dispel.

Ecumenical Armenia

The Patriarch of Moscow, Aleksy II, one of the principal agents of ecumenism in Europe, said in Graz that "the notion of ecumenism in the consciousness of most of our people implies something dangerous and absolutely unacceptable"...

I understand him well, and I think that it is a question of developing the awareness of our followers, of dispelling that fear and mistrust. Recently, I was saying to my friend Konrad Raiser, the General Secretary of the World Council of Churches, that we must launch an intense effort in the domain of an *ecumenical pastoralia*: the task of interpreting ecumenism in the real-life situations of our followers, our parishes, our dioceses. Ecumenism is still an affair of the elite, and has not yet affected the people of the Church. That is why we must sensitize them to it. We must explain that ecumenism is not completely foreign to our Christian tradition because in all Orthodox churches, we have had ecumenical experiences and figures.

Since I must limit myself to talking about my Armenian Church, I would like to emphasize the fact that it is without doubt one of the most open and ecumenical Eastern churches. For a long time, I have studied this aspect of our Church's history and I wrote a short essay entitled *Cilicia, or Ecumenical Armenia*, published in Paris by the CNRS in the book *The Kingdom of Cilicia*. Recently I gave a lecture on that theme at the Martin Luther University of Halle-Wittenberg, in which I tried to show that throughout our history, beginning in the fifth century, the ecumenical spirit has never left the experience of the Christian faith in Armenia. In different periods, we have maintained our fraternal contact with the Syriac and Greek churches, the churches of Alexandria, Antioch, Caesarea in Cappadocia, Constantinople, the Georgian Church, and, most importantly, after the Crusades, with the Roman Catholic Church. This shows us that for Armenia ecumenism is not necessarily a recent phenomenon, imported from somewhere else. That is why in this *pastoralia*, we must present ecumenism for what it is, emanating from our history and from the real experience of our Orthodox churches.

Another cause for the reservation or even opposition to ecumenism from certain sectors of the Orthodox churches is that in the meetings of the ecumenical movement, there were too many themes that did not relate to the everyday lives of our followers. Often, these meetings are a replica of the meetings of a parliament or a congress on sociology. Political, sociological and other problems, which are not in the domain of the churches' immediate vocation, have taken a significant position in many ecumenical organizations' activities. Of course, the churches cannot ignore the problems of the world, as I have said several times in our interviews. However, we must approach the problems of our world with a *distinctly Christian* attitude, and that attitude must be very visible to our followers.

What is also happening now is that certain specific problems concerning one particular church or region of the planet are presented as universal. For example, the sacerdotal ordination of women is not a fundamentally important issue for the faithful of our Eastern churches, and they cannot ask us to adopt, in this artificial manner, a specific problem that belongs to other churches by presenting it as universal and by forcing us to consider it in the ecumenical context. For us Orthodox churches, the World Council of

Churches and every other ecumenical organization must reflect the issues linked to the rediscovery of the churches' unity, since that is the principal *raison d'être* of the ecumenical movement.

Finally, there is a psychological cause for the anxiety caused by ecumenism, which is the fear of losing one's identity. That is a very tricky problem. Many of the negative reactions are caused by that fear, which is not openly expressed, but has roots that run very deep. Some Orthodox churches fear that our participation in the ecumenical movement will make us lose our Orthodox and Eastern specificity, our uniqueness, and even affect the orthodoxy of our churches.

Identity and distinctiveness

But how can we move beyond that fear and those prejudices concerning ecumenism?

It is precisely here that the *ecumenical pastoralia* is so very important. We must do everything possible to clearly show everyone that ecumenism is hardly a betrayal of our traditions.

In theological thought and in pastoral predication, it is obvious that we are obligated to reflect more on identity and distinctiveness now. I think that *identity* and *distinctiveness* are two modes of existence that are not contradictory. If someone does not know who he is, if he does not know himself deeply, then he cannot have a dialogue with others, he is lost from the beginning of the conversation. My Christian Armenian identity is so deeply rooted in my being that I can only think from within that category. But that specific identity must be seen in the context of a larger identity, which I call the *Christ-like identity*. Personally, when I pray with an Orthodox person, a Catholic or a Protestant, I never feel that my Armenian identity prevents me from being profoundly with the other person. In the prayer that we share, I transcend my specific identity without losing it, and I even reinforce it because it is flourishing in the common Christ-like identity. The Christ-like identity includes the recognition of diversity because it is part of God's creation.

The complementarity between identity and distinctiveness that you just illustrated might be the key to understanding that unity in Christ is never uniformity.

Sometimes in ecumenical dialogue, people understand the unity of faith as a "minimal agreement" on the fundamental truths of the Christian doctrine. Some think that we must take a step back, to the times when Christians were united. That implies going back to the sixteenth century to erase the separation of Catholics and Protestants, back to the eleventh century to undo the schism between the Christian East and West, to the fifth century to rediscover unity with the non-Chalcedonians…

People often talk about the undivided Church of the first centuries. But we must ask ourselves about exactly what this expression signifies. Does it mean that in the early centuries, there was no tension, no conflict, no diversity or variety? From the first years of its life, the Church has known a diversity of opinions and even oppositions. In the New Testament we see clearly that the apostles were very different from one another. Even during Christ's life, they argued about their primacy.... But those divergences and oppositions were always resolved through mutual understanding, in love and in the sense of belonging to the same Christ. We should reread, more often and with open spirits, the passage of Saint Paul's First Epistle to the Corinthians (1 Cor 1:10-13), in which the sense of belonging to Christ is uttered as a means to move beyond those divisions.

Saint Paul and Saint Peter did not think the same way about several issues, and the Council of Jerusalem in AD 49 had to resolve their dispute over the problem of Christians coming from the Hellenistic tradition who could not submit themselves to the traditions of believers living in the Jewish milieu. Then, the theological quarrels of the first centuries were just as difficult as the problems being posed today in the ecumenical movement.

So many theologians and hierarchs often say that unity does not mean uniformity. Unity is the sense of belonging to the same Christ, the only Son of God the Father in communion with the Holy Spirit, for all those who preach the same Gospel, and bear witness to it through their lives. If in diversity we can maintain that shared feeling of belonging to the Lord, then that implies that unity is real. A diversity consisting of nuances in the expression of the Christian faith is legitimate.

What you are saying is closely akin to what Pope John Paul II says in his book Crossing the Threshold of Hope, *that it is necessary that "the human species attains unity through plurality, that it learns to be a single Church in the pluralism of its forms of thought and action, of culture and civilization."*

Moments of glory and moments of crisis

Let's get back to the objective difficulties that exist right now in the Orthodox churches' participation in the ecumenical movement, most notably the World Council of Churches. How can they be resolved? What path could ecumenism take other than the World Council of Churches?

I think that the only way to resolve these problems is and will always be dialogue. I am not for despair or resignation; I am convinced that there where we find marked divergences, there is no other Christian way than dialogue, consisting of mutual respect and the patience that Jesus has shown with everyone.

Ecumenism is a general movement for unity and people must do everything to protect this common effort. People should not talk about different "ecumenisms" because there is only the single solicitude for the unity of the Church, which is expressed in rather different organizations and manifestations. It is in this context that we must also look at the World Council of Churches, which is the most representative ecumenical organization on the global level. Thus, instead of theorizing or envisioning possible solutions to replace the World Council, I think that we must deepen and intensify our dialogue on the nature and the scope of Orthodox participation.

The World Council of Churches is involved today in a process of reflection and trying to find a common definition of its positions, its structure and its goals. This is a task undertaken with the participation of the Orthodox churches, and I hope that there will be at least some Catholic observers so that the dialogue will be complete.

We of the Orthodox churches must not start from a position of weakness or fear. I think that for us, it is a duty to
be an integral part of the ecumenical movement. The current challenges come at a time when we are becoming
aware of the specificity of the Orthodox churches' contri-
butions, and we must persist, for the well being of the
Church and the world.

*The ecumenical movement is a phenomenon of this century. The
World Missionary Conference of Edinburgh in 1910 and the
Conference of Lausanne in 1927 cleared the way for the system-
atic dialogue among the churches. After the Second World War,
there was great interest in ecumenism, initially from Protestants
and members of Orthodox churches. In the 1950s, it was primarily the World Council of Churches, created in 1948 at the Conference of Amsterdam, that developed ecumenism. The 1960s,
with the Second Vatican Council and the meetings of Paul VI
and Athenagoras marked a profound change in the relationship
between the Catholic Church and other denominations. All
throughout the 1970s and '80s, interdenominational theological
dialogue continued developing, with the numerous mixed commissions and the ecumenical assemblies, until the great European Assembly of 1989 in Basel. The last decade has seen the
dialogue between the churches begin to slow down, and today,
ecumenism generally seems to be in crisis.*

*What do you, as one of its principal agents, think about the
current state of ecumenism?*

I am convinced that ecumenism is not a temporary phenomenon, and that in spite of the difficulties that exist, it
will continue to develop. The ecumenical movement is

facing a challenge today. At the beginning of the century, and even more after the ravages of the Second World War, the pioneers of ecumenism developed a vision of future unity that would be expressed enthusiastically. Soon thereafter, theological studies developed. In our century, we have experienced, so-to-speak, glorious moments of ecumenism. Now a new challenge is presenting itself. The world has changed, and we no longer live in the post-war world in which the World Council of Churches was formed, nor in the circumstances of the assemblies of New Delhi, Uppsala, Nairobi, Vancouver, just to mention the four in which I had the pleasure of personally participating. The world is constantly changing. How do we face these changes? I think that all of the churches engaged in the ecumenical movement must take the issue of showing the Christian way of approaching the problems of our era very seriously. We are often incapable of concretely resolving the evils of our world, but we must determine the Christian way of finding solutions. Here it is the specificity of our contribution that is important. Our Lord did not resolve all the problems of His time, but at the price of the cross, He never ceased to show His position and infinite solicitude.

A fundamental moment for ecumenism in the relationship between Orthodox Christians and Catholics took place in the 1960s. In 1964, in Jerusalem, Pope Paul VI and the Patriarch of Constantinople Athenagoras embraced for the first time, after nine centuries of separation. On July 25 and October 26, 1967, they repeated the same gesture in Saint George's Orthodox Cathedral in Istanbul and in Saint Peter's Basilica in Rome. The reciprocal excommunications of 1054 were annulled by Paul VI and Athenagoras on December 7, 1965, the day before the closing of the Second Vatican Council.

You were a witness to these events; what were your impressions?

Those gestures were great moments for the ecumenical movement; those events left an indelible imprint on contemporary history. Personally, I was delighted, spiritually strengthened, being present at that historic accolade of two great pastors in Jerusalem, the city of the Divine Pastor. After that historic meeting, Paul VI came to the Armenian Patriarchate in Jerusalem, and I was our Patriarch's interpreter. The cancellation of the anathema of 1054 was a crucially important symbolic gesture. When leaders of the Church can transcend dogmatic differences, that can only be reflected in all of the lives of their churches. But they were prophetic gestures in that it is natural that their followers need time to understand them and to translate them into everyday life.

From Basel to Graz: tearing down walls and building bridges

In Europe, people have noted that there is a great difference between the two ecumenical gatherings of 1989 in Basel and 1997 in Graz. The meeting in Basel occurred on the eve of the fall of the Berlin Wall and the entire continent was in a state of euphoria and optimism, created by Gorbachev's era. In Graz, the general feeling was veiled in a sort of deception. The historical situation became more difficult for Europe, and many expectations were not met, as the Patriarch of Moscow Aleksy II empha-

sized. Andrea Riccardi, the president of the community of Saint Egidio, observed:

> *In 1989 in Basel, there were two Europes before the fall of the Wall. Today that wall no longer exists. But there are many other walls.... The walls between the churches have become even higher.*

On the other hand, in Graz, the greatest agent of the Assembly was the people, the lay people. There were clearly more of them than in Basel; there were a great number of participants from Eastern Europe (one thousand from Romania), and from traditionally Catholic countries (Italy, Spain) who in the past rarely participated in ecumenical initiatives. Could we say that while ecumenism has been accompanied by difficulties at the level of church officials, at the level of the people, it has become more spontaneous?

First, I must say that I cannot make a comparison between the two European ecumenical assemblies for the simple reason that I did not personally participate in the Basel Assembly.

Graz was for me a great manifestation of the signs of the time. It is true, today the Berlin Wall no longer exists, but the destruction of walls does not yet imply communion. We must build bridges between the churches, and it is much easier and faster to destroy a wall than to build a bridge. So Graz gave me great hope because there, I saw bridges already in construction. First of all, the cooperation between the Conference of European Churches and the Council of European Catholic Episcopal Conferences was very important. In spite of the difficulties that presented themselves, it was a great lesson in fraternal coop-eration. Orthodox Christians, Catholics, Protestants, all proved their desire to manifest the Christian faith in the extremely secularized world that Europe is today. As you said, in Graz, there were a very large number of partici-pants, especially laypeople, young people and women. That participation is in itself a fundamental contribution to ecumenism on the continent. Graz was a testimonial to the vitality and the importance of charismatic movements; the churches must take the people very seriously, the people who are demonstrating well-formed Christian consciences, but who need to be encouraged by the hierarchy. Thus, the gathering for me was a very promising beginning for the future of Europe.

Also, the meetings of young people that followed the assembly of Graz, under the patronage of the Pope, spon-sored by Taize, in Paris and in Munich, with hundreds of thousands of participants, gave me great joy and made me more confident about the future.

Personally, I am always more convinced that the prin-cipal task of everyone who wished to engage in ecu-menism is to build new bridges between our churches, our traditions and our cultures.

Dogmatic divergences, psychological differences

I would like to talk about a specific aspect of ecumenism in order to learn about the dialogue between Catholics and Orthodox Christians.

Although these two churches are very close in terms of their doctrines — they share all the sacraments, the apostolic succes-

sion (which they recognize mutually), their tradition and a large part of their ecclesiastical discipline – the dialogue between Catholics and Orthodox Christians is paradoxically more difficult than the dialogue between Catholics and Protestants.

Would the psychological and cultural barrier, which marks the difference between the East and the West of Europe, offer more resistance than dogmatic barriers?

I think that the history of interrelation between Catholics and Orthodox Christians is longer and more complicated than that of the relationship between Catholics and Protestants. Furthermore, we must not forget that Protestantism was born from Catholicism, and that was in a relatively recent period. So it is natural that there would be an affinity between the mentalities and lives of the Catholic and Protestant peoples.

Between Orthodox Christians and Catholics, cultural and psychological differences, as you said, are much more profound than the dogmatic divergences. That situation is an illustration of what we call in the ecumenical movement the "non-theological factors" of division.

In our memory of the relationship between Catholicism and Orthodoxy, there is a fundamental problem, inherited from the past, but which remains very troublesome: the problem of the missions the Catholic Church organized in the Christian East, which that engendered the Eastern Catholic churches. That created a psychological barrier that, for an Orthodox Christian, is difficult to overcome. When these churches were formed, ecclesiology and the general current of theological thought, in Rome and elsewhere, were very different from those of today; also, people did not know each other very well, and that caused many misunderstandings.

Today, with the progress made in the domain of ecumenism and mutual understanding, we have arrived at a new way of seeing unity — which does not imply *uniatism*. The Catholic Church must be vigilant and not fall into the old ways of trying to turn Orthodox Christians into Catholics, in the name of the unity of the Church. That is a part of the mutual love and respect that we must show, in a world for which it is not the form of one's faith that is in question, but faith itself.... I know that, officially, the Catholic Church does not approve of proselytism and renounces it, since this is stated openly in many of its declarations. But today, we still see signs, vestiges of that old mentality. The task of eliminating those vestiges to clear the path toward unity must be reciprocal. That allows us to hope that these non-theological factors of division will diminish with time.

If the barrier between Catholics and Orthodox Christians is not only dogmatic — maybe not so dogmatic — but rather cultural, psychological, etc., then we should look for unity in these areas before anywhere else. One of the reasons for a certain crisis in the dialogue between the two churches today is that ecumenism is practiced almost exclusively on the theological level. To move beyond prejudices, reciprocal offenses, a deeper mutual understanding and an exchange on the level of the people would be important...

Allow me to cite an example from my personal experience. In my childhood, the Catholic religious education I received in Italy only gave me vague mental representations of other

Christian denominations, as is often the case for believers in countries where one church is a clear majority. Then, having lived in Switzerland for seven years, I had the fortune to know the Reformed churches and especially the Orthodox church. That truly affected me, not only because it showed me the beauty of these churches, but because it gave me a new approach to several issues concerning faith. That is why I wonder if in the ecumenical dialogue between the Orthodox and Catholic churches, we should not give more weight to that reciprocal exchange between followers.

I think so. In recent times, we have made great progress in the area of theological dialogue. My ecumenical experience has convinced me that we must extend the dialogue to other spheres, beyond purely theological studies, affecting only dogmatic differences. To clear away these psychological and historical obstacles, we must direct the dialogue to a broader context, embodying the totality of the aspects of Christian life. We must move from mutual understanding to trust, to feeling of our shared belonging to Christ, to serve Him together in humanity.

I do not want to reduce the importance of theological dialogue, since our differences, although they may be primarily cultural and psychological, are also dogmatic, and they must be clarified on the level of theological reflection. But today we must recognize ourselves in the concrete experience of the communion of the Christian faith in spite of dogmatic differences. That is why, without underestimating the potential of numerous theological commissions, consultations and conversations, we must not limit our ecumenical commitment to these things, since Christian life, while it is founded on dogmas, goes infinitely beyond them. There are other aspects of a life of faith that we must take much more seriously, which we have not in ecumenical dialogue.

You were talking about the exchange between Catholics and Orthodox Christians. I think that a continual communication is necessary: undertaking common works, performing services together. You are familiar with the words that Jesus spoke to Philip: "If you do not believe my words, believe at least in the cause of these works" (Jn 14:11). In Christian life, work is the test, the verification, the *proof* of the truth. The common engagement of the churches and the mutual sharing of their resources are a dimension that will play a determinant role in the process of purifying the pan-Christian environment.

Proselytism and uniatism

In the last decade, the countries of the former Soviet Union and other countries of Eastern Europe seem to have experienced a wave of foreign missionaries. The Orthodox churches of these countries have begun to talk about Catholic and Protestant proselytism again. Aside from the proselytism of sects and independent churches, in your opinion, is there proselytism from traditional Protestant churches and the Catholic Church in Armenia today?

I would like to respond to your direct question with a yes and a no, and I assure you that this is not a diplomatic response! The fact is that there are cases where proselytism is open and manifest, and others where it is latent and not easily identified.

Our Catholic and Protestant brothers assure us that they are not pursuing such a policy, and I have no reason to doubt them. But the situation is very complex and everything depends on the definition that you give to proselytism. We have just come out of a situation of seventy years of religious stagnation, in which belonging to the Church was different than in the past. Many people were not baptized because that was an act that could have led to unpleasant consequences. Others rarely went to church for the same reason and because the entire system of parishes was eliminated.

Now, some of our brothers from the Armenian Protestant and Armenian Catholic churches believe that these people, not having been formally linked to our Church, can be baptized as Catholics or Protestants without it being considered an act of proselytism. Personally, I think that this is a manifestation of proselytism because there is a sense of non-formal belonging to our Church, which has always given form to our nation's faith. Armenians generally have an unwavering feeling of belonging to their Mother Church, which they consider the nation's Church. People should not attack a feeling so profound and unshakable, a feeling that has survived centuries of historical vicissitudes.

Our Protestant Armenian and Catholic Armenian brothers have suffered injustices and persecutions in the time of Communism, and we can and must remedy that; we have no objection there. But that argument must not be used to defend the use of proselytism, even in a less obvious form. I will repeat what I have already said, that today it is not the *form* of one's faith that is in question, but faith itself. So instead of trying to "win over" people to your own denomination, other Christians should help the church of the country to pursue its task of preaching and service, by putting aside what might cause a new spiritual confusion.

Our Church has served the people for the last seventeen centuries. I believe that creating parallel or competing structures does not makes any sense. Today, Armenia is coming out of a sort of torpor, and as always, that moment of awakening is delicate and important. We must not lose this opportunity by preaching with a narrow denominational attitude. No one will win anything from this competition.

Now we are coming to another tricky problem in ecumenism: uniatism. Let us limit ourselves to what concerns Armenia: the Armenian Catholic Church. How do you view Armenian Catholics? Are they in competition with your church? What would you like to say about the Armenian Protestant church?

Today in Armenia, the competition in the engagement and service of Christ is unjustifiable. It is also necessary to say that often people do not speak of competition, and it does not exist openly; but competition has taken form, so to speak, by itself, in the people's perception.

In any case, the issue of competition is not for me the most important one. The fundamental problem is that we must give our people today the evidence of a Christian church in which, in spite of the difference inherited from the past, we can present ourselves through common undertakings. When the people see, in this or that concrete task, that our Mother Church has dedicated itself to working with the participation of our Catholic and Protestant brothers, then that gives more credibility to our message. On the other hand, when Catholic and Protestant Armenians pursue their own goals, separated from the Apostolic Church, believers can only perceive that as a sort of competition, which will surely be beneficial neither to the Church of Christ, nor for our new Armenia.

Is there currently in Armenia cooperation of this kind? Do you have a relationship with the Catholic or Protestant Armenians?

Yes, there is a relationship. Their representatives come to visit us here at Holy Etchmiadzin. I have myself visited an Armenian Catholic Church in the north of our country and I attended the one hundred fiftieth anniversary of the Armenian Evangelical Church and addressed a message of paternal love to them. However, there is not yet a well-defined program for our working together.

We have some concrete experiences of working with the Church of Rome and the Protestant churches of different countries. I would like to mention two examples of that fraternal collaboration. One is the hospital of Ashotsk, in the North of Armenia, established by the Italian *Caritas*, with the blessings of Pope John Paul II. It is an exemplary institution in the service of the sick, in which there is absolutely no denominational discrimination. Some representatives from our Church are a part of the managing committee of the hospital, and they work in close and continual collaboration. The other example is a factory for prefabricated construction materials, established in Armenia right after the earthquake by the great German

Protestant organization *Diakonisches Werk*. That, too, was an experience of ecumenical cooperation. Recently our German brothers and sisters have handed over that enterprise to our Church, which has taken charge of it.

These are the concrete cases in which we have been able to demonstrate the unity of faith beyond dogmatic differences in the service of the people. I think that in the future, we must work a lot to prepare and cultivate this type of cooperation.

Kerigma, koïnonia, diakonia

Until today, ecumenism has primarily followed two paths: that of symbolic gestures between the heads of churches (such as the embrace of Paul VI and Athenagoras), and that of the theological dialogue of numerous commissions. The first has had the effect of disturbing the wall of indifference and prejudices. The second has clarified many of the relative problems with fundamental truths in doctrine by giving ecumenism a scholarly solidity.

Today, we may have reached a point at which it is difficult for the heads of churches to make gestures that are more significant than those already made; theological dialogue, on the other hand, does not touch upon other, more important points, and runs the risk of being reduced to a sterile discussion between experts.... Facing these problems, several figures committed to the ecumenical movement for a long time think that they should find a new spiritual content for ecumenism. Cardinal Martini said in Graz that we should "find a strong, inspiring and coordinating idea," and Chiara Lubich outlined the details of an "ecumenical spirituality."

What is your position on this subject?

During our interviews, I have already referred to the spiritual content of ecumenism. Here I would like to cite Abbot Paul Couturier and his "spiritual ecumenism," which had so fascinated me from the very beginning of my ecumenical engagement. I think that if we lose the spiritual dimension of ecumenism, we become simple interlocutors who exchange points of view without arriving at an existentially valuable conclusion. Without that spirituality, all of our efforts in theological dialogue will have no tangible results because the ecumenical movement's task is not to conduct scholarly research; after all, it is not a question here of a theological institute.

There are two dimensions without which these purely theological conversations concerning dogmatism will not lead to concrete results. Those two dimensions are the spiritual and the social. You were talking about spirituality. If in our ecumenical dialogue, we neglect our sense of belonging to the same Christ and our constant quest to reinforce our spiritual bond, by praying for one another and with one another, then ecumenism becomes a work characterized by theoretical and scholarly research that could be conducted, and probably better, by many scholarly institutions.

The other dimension, which people seldom talk about, consists in giving a concrete expression to the ecumenical spirit and applying it to everyday life. I realize more and more that if there is no common action that affects the reality of people's lives, then we fall back into the temptation of separating the spiritual from the material, which goes against both Christ's spirit and a sound theology.

I think that ecumenism must consider at the same time three aspects of Christian life: *koïnonia*, the aspect of spiritual communion, *kerigma*, preaching, and *diakonia*, service. Often we speak of *koïnonia*, of communion with God and with others. That communion is not only a feeling or an idea, but a way of living that embodies action and service. The gospels show us that in the ministry of Christ, prayer, teaching and service were always inseparably intertwined. Thus the ecumenical movement must rediscover these three dimensions: the spirit, the intellect and service. Only the interrelation of these three components of Christian life can give us a healthy, promising ecumenism for today and tomorrow.

Finally, I believe from the deepest part of my soul that in spite of our current condition of division, the *One* Church, the Church of Christ, exists in all of the churches. It is in my church, yours, in so many others. We must rediscover the sense of our common belonging to the *One* Church, which our Fathers had when the churches of Alexandria, Antioch, Rome, etc., already existed; the members of these churches all recognize themselves as the offspring of the same Church of Christ.

The issue is to rediscover that unity and bring it back to life, on the basis of the fundamentals that comprised it in the first centuries, by dispelling the fog that history has created around it.

❧ CHAPTER X ❧

Suffering

Suffering and the chosen people

Your Holiness, Armenia is an ancient land that has a long and glorious history. But the long chronicle of its history contains many pages of suffering. Armenia has always been at odds with unfriendly neighbors, who have devastated, pillaged, destroyed. Your people have known very different kinds of domination: the Romans, the Arabs, the Ottomans, the Turks, the Tartars, the Russians.... As the historian Gibbon says, from the dawn of its history your country was a theater of perpetual war. More than once, you have seen the horrible experience of genocide, the bitterness of deportation, diaspora, a dividing country.... In the last century, Armenians from the mother country experienced seventy years of Communism.

Finally, a very frequent element in your history is natural catastrophes, primarily earthquakes.

In short, Armenia's history has known its share of sadness.

What role has this destiny of suffering had on your culture and your national character?

The experience of suffering that we have lived through could not have happened without marking our mentality, our national being. In the Armenian culture, we have certain imprints left by that suffering, of which the most evident might be the melancholy that has affected our music and literature, so rich with elegies and lamentations.

But there is also the flip side of the coin. That suffering has actually created in Armenians the attitude that we must react, which has nothing to do with resignation or passivity, and which you could characterize as tenacity, perseverance, endurance. That is one of the traits of our character: a quality, resulting from what we have experienced in life, which makes me think of Saint Paul's words to the Romans: "We celebrate even in our suffering because we know that suffering produces patience, patience produces resistance, and resistance produces hope" (Rom 5:3-4). The sufferings of history were a test for the Armenians, a sort of challenge, to which they reacted not only by *enduring* that suffering, but also by *transcending* it through a surprising creativity. That national characteristic has been recognized several times and made evident by foreign chroniclers and visitors in different eras.

I would like to add a remark to these considerations. Often, suffering has been seen by historians, Armenian or not, as such a dominant aspect of our history that the very name Armenia is inseparably associated with suffering. The theologian and liturgist Archdale King said: "The historiography of Armenia is a synonym for martyrology." While speaking of our martyrs in his history of the Church, the French academic Daniel-Rops uses the expression "bleeding Armenia," but adds subsequently the adjective "living." I think that those two adjectives together offer a good definition: suffering has given our people the spirit to not resign themselves to death—to their disappearance. Thus, as paradoxical as it may seem, suffering has contributed to the development of the creativity of our people.

That is why, in going back to our literature, next to the numerous elegies to which I alluded, one of the major literary genres is the epic, which celebrates heroism.

The experience of persecution, genocide and dispersion makes your history similar to that of the Jewish people. For the Jewish people, the destiny of suffering is inextricably linked to being chosen by God.

So is your destiny a tragic fatality, a condemnation from the Eternal One? Or do the Armenian people feel that, because of their history, they are a chosen people?

I think that in our people's psychology, that sense of being chosen does not have a place. Of course, historical facts make our fate similar to that of the Jewish people. But the circumstances of the suffering in Armenian history can be principally explained through geopolitical factors, through the geographical position of our country, which, situated at the crossroads of the great powers of antiquity, was used as a *buffer state*.

One part of the persecution we endured was because of our Christian faith. Our neighbors, not being Christian and understanding that our tenacity came from our faith, sought to suppress the source of our identity and tenacity, beginning with the Mazdeans from Sassanid Iran and up through the events of our century, for example the genocide. The genocide was a well-organized attempt to suppress our national Christian identity in the heart of the Turkish state, which wanted to be a pan-Turkic Muslim state. We should add to that that certain Christian powers with a colonizing spirit acted in the same manner, in trying to assimilate our people and to submit us to their monolithic and absolute domination, while undermining our Church's independence. I am alluding here to a certain policy of the Byzantine Empire, to the attempts of the Crusaders and even to some of the attitudes of the Russian Empire.

But to return to your question, I can say that the idea of being chosen, or the awareness of being a chosen people, exists neither in our literature, nor in our culture.

The proof of our freedom

If there is not the idea of being a chosen people, there might be a sort of idea of predestination. When one looks at your history of suffering, it is easy to think that God or History has been running a hard and cruel scientific experiment on your people, a sort of survival test. The result of that test is that in spite of the worst conditions of life, your people have not only survived, but have created a more interesting and original civilization and culture.

For a believer, these circumstances are not due to chance, but to God, who wishes them or allows them to exist. Did God wish a fate of suffering on you?

You may have noticed that in responding to your question on suffering, I did not use the word "survive." People often say that our people have survived the episodes of our history. But we have not only survived! We have done much more than that: we have lived our history as actors, with a great creativity in the area of culture. We have not lived simply to let life pass us by, but to live fully with values that transcend time and space. Our history could be an illustration of what used to be said in Latin: *Vita non est vivere, sed valere* ("Life is not living but having value").

In any case, we must not consider our case of suffering as being unique; suffering is common to the history of many nations. God has allowed this suffering not only for our people but for many others around us; the Assyrians, for example, have suffered as much as we, and also the Georgians, the Russians and in the past, the Tartars...

I think that in our reading of God's will, we can say that God *allows* suffering, but we cannot say that God *provokes* suffering. Simply, suffering is a part of the human condition; but God always gives us the opportunity to transcend suffering, to vanquish death through life.

So sadness is inherent to humanity. In the narrative of Genesis, sadness appears in Creation as a consequence of sin. After the Fall, God says to the woman: "I will increase the suffering of your pregnancies, and you will give birth in pain." To the man, He says: "It is with great toil that you will obtain food from the earth for all the days of your life... It is through the sweat of your brow that you will eat bread" (Gn 3:16-19). Thus, that implies that suffering is like an attack on the product of Creation, that because of sin, we are condemned to crawl through our existence.

Sadness is a result of sin, of the distancing from God, since the presence of God in our souls and in our conscience is a source of joy, the force for our victory over sadness. But there is also a positive side to sadness. We must look at what suffering provokes in us. I think that it makes us more authentically human. It makes us rediscover the right relationship with God. How many times do we forget to thank God for all of His gifts? Only sadness makes us turn ourselves toward Him.

Suffering can become purification. That can clearly be seen in the lives of the saints. It makes us understand what true spiritual and human values are, the values that are here for eternity. It is the experience of suffering that teaches us the difference between happiness and pleasure; too often, the people of our time confuse those two concepts.

So our consumer society is always looking to run from and to exorcise suffering. But on the contrary, you are saying that suffering, our inheritance from sin, is necessary to us, because it makes us more human...

Pirandello, the Italian writer from the start of the twentieth century, who was not close to the Christian faith, said that man "is never as human as when he suffers; because he wants to see the reason for his suffering, to understand what causes it, and to see if it is fair. But when he is happy, he does not ask himself a single question and takes that joy as if it were due to him..."

I think that sadness shows us the profound meaning of life and makes us understand that we are not the masters of everything, but rather the admirers—and I would even say the servers—of Creation. What I am saying here is also from personal experience. Often, when I have experienced moments of suffering or illness, life has taken on a much greater meaning, which I have never perceived while happy and in good health. Before a hospital bed and a coffin, I "tasted" the value of life as I have nowhere else, since it is death and sadness that make us understand the value of life.

But there is yet another positive aspect to suffering. Suffering does not come to us directly from God; on the contrary, how much misery and sadness in life is created by ourselves, one to another. Now, if we believe that God gave us freedom, that means that we have the opportunity to choose, and that in that choice we can fail, be mistaken, and consequently suffer or make others suffer. That implies that man's dignity and specificity includes suffering. Suffering is the proof of our freedom; the very fact that it exists tells us that God respects our freedom and dignity. If suffering did not exist, we would be robots.

"Why?"

One of the most beautiful works of poetry in ancient Armenian literature is the Elegies *by Gregory of Narek, the* Book of Songs of Sadness. *The theme is that of suffering, reprised from the Book of Job.*

In the Bible, Job is the model of the man who suffers not because of his sins, but because God is testing him. It is the great theme of the suffering of a person who is good — the most troubling and tragic human question: why is there sadness, why is there suffering?

The *Elegies*, or *Lamentations*, of Saint Gregory of Narek are rather different from the Book of Job. In these elegies, there is a very profound interior drama, the drama of all men.

Saint Gregory represented the spiritual struggle of a man who feels that he has the infinity and the all-powerfulness of God and, at the same time, sees the human pettiness that leads him to sin. It is the conflict between the desire to elevate yourself toward God, to participate in His grace, and our condition of fragility; the interior turmoil between the taste for the divine, or the aspiration toward God, and the seduction of sin, or the attraction of the Earth. Finally, that inner struggle becomes prayer.

That situation is rather different from what is presented to us in the Book of Job, which is focused on the theme of the test and on the dialogue, inner dialogue and dialogue with God, of a man who suffers because he does not understand why it exists.

Believers explain the suffering of good people with the idea of the test. But does a God who is love truly have the right to put His friends to the test?

I think it does not make any sense to ask if God *has the right*. God has all rights. He goes infinitely beyond our intelligence, and what seems to us today to be a tragedy might become a source of happiness tomorrow. A father who corrects his son is not always understood by his child, who might have the feeling of not being loved. But over the years, the son will be grateful to the father for having made him suffer.

Often we make the mistake of thinking of and judging divine action from within our own experience; but we cannot judge God with purely human criteria.

"Where were you when I founded the Earth?" At the end of the Book of Job, God, who had remained in silence to watch his suffering, asks Job this ironic question. The question, and a long series of similar ones, is the only explanation that God gives Job for the test. That implies what you just said: God in His all-powerfulness and wisdom goes completely beyond us; His designs are completely incomprehensible to us. Faith certainly consists in accepting with confidence what comes from God, even when it does not conform to our plans, our desires, our logic.

Don't we even have the right to ask God for explanations, to look for a meaning in this suffering?

I think that asking about the meaning of suffering is the oldest and most profound human question, and I would even say the most justified. God is love and the source of happiness. Why does he allow us to suffer? In its literature, our people have asked themselves this question and have protested against certain circumstances, even ending up revolting against them. How many times in his life does every man ask himself that question again?

However that question will remain with us, since if we could fully understand the meaning of divine acts, we would be gods. That does not imply fatalism. I only think that the reason for suffering is not explicable in terms of logic. On the other hand, we know how to get through the test, how to avoid succumbing to it.

Each time that someone asks me the question, "Why is there suffering?" "Why is there sadness?" I feel an inner embarrassment because I cannot find a logical or scientific answer to that question. I am familiar with suffering, I experience it and, like every man, I try to go beyond it, sometimes without success. But I have no logical explanation for its existence. I think that in reality that question has an existential character and thus must be approached in an individual manner, by giving it a personal response.

One of the questions that have occupied minds in the second half of our century concerns the reason for pogroms. Why the Holocaust in Auschwitz? Why the genocide of Armenians in 1915, where a million and a half of your fellow citizens were exterminated?

Those questions do not have definitive answers. In our time, maybe as never before, man has shown how far his brutality can go. Very recently an American writer in *Time* magazine characterized ours as a "century of genocide." Recently, people have been talking a lot about the murderous attitude of man, to which they have given a definition that surprises with its play on words: "Man's inhumanity to humanity."

At the same time, I think that even where these monstrous excesses of human evil in our era are concerned, there is light beyond the shadows. The Holocaust and everything done against the Jewish people by fascism was humanly abominable; but we must also emphasize the expressions of solidarity and sympathy that the people have received over the course of the century. Even during the pogroms, there were people who opposed the extermination, sometimes at the price of their own lives. I am very happy about the recent recognition and condemnation of the genocide perpetrated against the Armenians in 1915. I see in it the expression of a certain sympathy toward our people.

I think that it is important that in our suffering, we also see the positive side to our human reality, which is always taking place in the context of that game between light and darkness. In our human lives, suffering and joy, sadness and happiness intermingle all the time, and we must prevent ourselves from seeing suffering as the dominant aspect.

At the lowest point of the test

Overall, man is good and wicked, and that explains at the same time his great generosity and his murderous madness. But if the answer to the question of why pogroms and wars exist is human wickedness, then what is the answer to why we have illnesses, cancer, AIDS? Why these natural catastrophes?

On December 7, 1988, at 11:41 a.m., the earth trembled in Spitak, located near the city of Leninakan in northern Armenia. Twenty-five thousand people lost their lives; five hundred thousand were left homeless; the town of Spitak was wiped off the map. It was one of the greatest natural catastrophes of our century. But the earthquake of 1988 was only the last, chronologically, of a very long series. From the beginning of your history, the chronicles relate earthquakes that have periodically devastated your country in 341, 735, 893, 1319, 1679, 1827, 1840, 1926. And those are only the dates of the most catastrophic earthquakes...

Why are there these natural catastrophes? Why the earthquake in Spitak?

I can only repeat that there are question to which our human intelligence does not have adequate answers...

I know well the extent to which that earthquake was a horrible calamity, an extremely difficult experience. I know how much suffering it caused, since I went to Leninakan, from Lebanon, ten days after the catastrophe. I saw with my own eyes the despair of the mothers looking for their children, the lines of coffins, the ruins, the piles of debris. At night, when I went back to Etchmiadzin, I was in a state of indescribable distress. But before that general destruction, I understood that we should not let ourselves be overcome with despair, that we had to react immediately to work on the reconstruction, which I said the next day in celebrating the Liturgy in the Cathedral of Holy Etchmiadzin. In this way, I found the strength to move on from that state of spiritual prostration.

I understand very well that when you lose a person who was dear to you, when you learn that someone has a fatal disease, you wonder why? But this question cannot be answered logically. There are many aspects of our lives that cannot be explained. When the clouds hide the sun, you don't really wonder why God is making it so; it is something that is a part of nature, part of the rhythm of life. Faith reveals itself precisely when our logic does not understand.

So the question of why the earthquake happened, or illnesses, remains without a logical response for us; here, it is a matter of believing that God is present even at the lowest point of the test.

So the question "Why" has no answer. All the same, it is human to ask that question. You have said that the question of why the innocent person suffers is the most profound human question.

In asking ourselves this question, we are showing our humanity, the same humanity that Christ assumed, who also asked Himself this tragic question. His cry — Eli, Eli, lama sabachthani — is the most sublime expression of that human question "Why": "My God, My God, why have you abandoned me?"

That is true. Christ experienced that moment of agony, which followed what happened to Him in the Garden of Gethsemane. But in both cases, He surpassed His despair. In Gethsemane, he prayed: "My Father, if it is possible, take this cup away from me." But then He resubmitted Himself to His Father's will: "Not what I want, but what you want. Let your will be done" (Mt 26:39-42). Similarly, on the cross, according to Luke's account, He said: "Father I return my spirit to your hands" (Lk 23:46).

The recognition and acceptance of God's will are not a humiliation for man. On the contrary, that voluntary submission makes the greatness of man, who through that act reaffirms his condition as God's creature, called to be in communion with his Creator.

Absence and presence

You are emphasizing trust in God, the fact of feeling His presence at the low point of the test.

A refrain of the Armenian vespers from Easter, reprised from Isaiah, says: "...because God is with us." "God, the Lord, is with us, know it O people, be defeated, because God is with us. Listen all over the earth: because God is with us. Strengthen yourselves, but you will be beaten because God is with us. [...] We will have no fear for you because God is with us..."

Where was God during the earthquake, the genocide, the dispersion? Did He abandon you to the test?

There are two levels of meeting with God in the test, which I have experienced in my life and which I clearly noted after the earthquake of 1988.

The first level is complete distress, even revulsion. You wonder where God is, you have the impression that he is absent. Such is the reaction when you are facing general destruction as in Spitak. But immediately after the earthquake, the demonstrations of solidarity with an unheard of generosity began to emerge: food, medications, clothing and other forms of help arrived from everywhere. Many men and women from every country came to Armenia to help look for bodies and to help in the reconstruction. Such generosity allowed us all to feel God's presence. That solidarity was the manifestation of true humanity, which is the influence of God: Love.

I think that it often happens like that. In these tests, there is always a moment of crisis, a moment when one experiences the absence of God. It is a matter of going beyond that moment of doubt and solitude, that moment of abandonment, through an act of faith and love. That is how you see that God is present—that He was always beside us, that He was there even in His absence.

Jesus on the cross might have experienced that feeling of the absence of God. Your Eastern spirituality emphasizes the concept of God's kenosis: all-powerful God, who, in order to take on a bodily form, enter into history and make Himself a man, reduces Himself, makes Himself small by limiting Himself to one era, one nation, etc. God's self-limitation reaches its summit on the cross in his cry of abandonment. The paradox of the cross is that Jesus, who is God, in that moment shares with us the feeling of God's absence...

Certainly. Christ's humanity was a full humanity because He shared all of the human condition, except for sin. He knew temptation in the desert, hunger, fatigue, doubt, and that cry of abandonment shows us that on the cross. He experienced first the feeling of God's absence, and then submitted Himself to His will.

That spiritual experience is not removed from everyday life because religion is not removed from everyday reality. That is why in our lives we continually experience those two feelings of the presence and absence of God.

But the cross, the place where Jesus experienced abandonment as the absence of God, is in reality the place *par excellence* of God's presence. The act of voluntarily accepting the Crucifixion for humanity's redemption, being the highest expression of sacrifice and thus of love, is for that very reason the place of the most complete presence of God, who is Love. That is why for us, too, the acceptance of suffering is an encounter with God. It is in this way that I understand the words of Saint Paul: "When I am weak, that is when I am strong" (2 Cor 12:10).

He turned Himself to us

The Crucifixion is without a doubt the most frequent subject of Armenian miniature art. The khatchkar, the cross sculpted in stone, is a dominant element in your art and in the landscape of your countryside.

Your Holiness, what is the cross — that "scandal for the Jews," that "madness for the pagans"?

Often, theologians, especially in the West, talk about the cross, about the theology of the cross; the cross has become something abstract, an idea, a theological concept. But the cross has no meaning without Christ crucified because it is the *Crucifixion*, the act of the Son of God allowing Himself to be nailed on a cross, that has redeemed us. It is the Crucifixion that gives the existential content to the theology of the cross.

The Crucifixion is the evidence of God's *kenosis*. God made Himself man and suffered; that is the greatness of Christianity...

...Someone said that the religion of God suffering is a religion of superior quality...

If God had not suffered, He would be for us a wise instructor who gives us lessons from high up in His chair. But God identified with us, His creatures, and through that, He showed us His essence — love — since love is always an identification with the person who is loved.

The cross is a sublime manifestation of love, which is God, and at the same time it is the proof of Jesus Christ's majesty. God turned toward man. In his letter to the Philippians (Phil 2:6-9), Saint Paul explains to us that Jesus Christ, who was God, became exactly like men, took on the condition of a servant and lived in humility until accepting His death on the cross; "That is why God raised Him," says the apostle, which means that the greatness of God passes through the humiliation of the cross.

Our God is not a God jealous of His majesty, who lives in an ivory tower in some seventh heaven. He is a God who uses His grandeur while being crucified through love. If you look at the fields of wheat before the harvest, you see that the ears of wheat that are full of grain bend, lean towards the ground; the ear that remains tall, vertical, is empty, is no more than straw... Thus God, who is the fullness of love, turned toward our emptiness, and showed His complete love in His crucified and abandoned Son.

Christ is risen!

To submit oneself to God's will, to feel that Christ suffered as we do, that He identified with our suffering... But what would you say, Holiness, to someone who had no faith and discovered that he was afflicted with cancer or AIDS?

I fear that I cannot say very much about that since, without faith, which gives you spiritual tenacity, I myself would not know what to do if faced with such situations. It is the same for my people. I think that without faith, they could not have faced so much suffering.

Thus I would try to stay close to that person, to make him feel my solidarity, my solicitude, my friendship, my full support.... In a word, I would try to share his sadness, since the Crucifixion, that extraordinary sharing that God made of our suffering and of our humanity, is also our capacity to love one another. To truly adore the cross means participating in Christ's Crucifixion through the sharing of others' suffering...

I know that many people in these situations, exactly when they have the feeling of having lost all support, have *rediscovered* in their heart a forgotten faith. The heart of the Christian faith is the Resurrection, the message that death is not the end of everything, since Christ defeated death. That faith animated the apostles, the first Christians and the martyrs, who through their faith confronted their persecutors until death. This is the great renewal of Christianity, which defies our logic.

I would like to cite an episode in our people's resistance against the Mazdean religion. In 451, the same year as the Council of Chalcedon, the "King of Kings" of the Mazdean Persian convened a meeting of the Armenian princes. At that time, they were allies in all of the battles that they fought against the barbarians from the northern Caucasus; Prince Vartan had even saved the king's life. So the king said to the Armenians, "How can you, so valiant and courageous, follow Jesus, who was so weak that He could not even defend Himself and get away from a few Jews?" The Armenians were stunned: "How do you know that story?" He answered, "I have ordered my Mazdean priests, the magi, to read your Scriptures to me." Then the youngest of the Armenian princes who, among others, was named Karekin, retorted, "You Majesty, why did you not ask your magi to continue reading? You would have seen that Jesus, who was crucified, *came back to life!*"

Christ is risen! That shocking, extraordinary announcement is the only sentence that I would address to someone facing death. We just spoke of why suffering exists. How much ink has been dedicated to that question, which has always occupied philosophers, poets and theologians? But all of those intellectual efforts have not led to a definitive and satisfying answer regarding the origin of evil, of suffering and death. Whatever the case may be, suffering and death are a part of the human condition that we cannot escape.

If a person does not believe in the Resurrection, death is truly the end of everything, the annihilation of a human person. The Christian believes that man can go beyond death because Christ has already defeated it. One of our theologians and historians of the fifth century, Yeghishé, said: "A death whose meaning is not understood is truly death; a death whose meaning is understood is immortality." God made it so that we were born on this earth, but our life does not end down here. Victor Hugo said that although the human body finds its final prison in its tomb, the soul has wings for eternity. Faith in the Resurrection has been the vital force of our people. That same faith still operates today, and will always remain for those who wish to follow Christ.

ᔓ CHAPTER XI ᔒ

Facing the Future

Makers of history

Your Holiness, in your address to the European Ecumenical Assembly in Graz, you said:

> The world changes. Change is not new. The world has always known change and it will continue to change. We are ourselves carried along with these changes. We are not the objects but the subjects, not the victims, but the actors.

In that continual process of change, of which progress is one of the most important elements, how do you see your times, our world today?

That is truly a vast and complex question, and I believe that one cannot adequately respond to it in just a few words. Nevertheless, I will try to show an aspect that seems to me to be specific to our times. I think that our world, over the course of the century, has seen, in general, some great scientific, technological, industrial, and eco-

269

nomic discoveries. And that was *in spite of* two World Wars, which created so many evils, so much suffering and desolation.

At the same time, when we talk about the world, we must first specify what we understand by that. Our modern world is not monolithic. Europe and the industrialized countries are another world in relation to less economically developed countries. I think that in wealthy countries, progress has given rise to a feeling of all-powerfulness in men; we are now capable of going to the moon, to Mars, of controlling the atom. All of that inspires in us the temptation of thinking that human life is sufficient unto itself. We believe that we are the masters of our lives. That is the direct cause of the exasperating secularism of our times, in which the presence of God is cast aside, marginalized and even eliminated.

On the other hand, many of our great intellectuals and scientists think that new scientific discoveries can show us just what a mystery this world is, that everything we know today is infinitely less than what we must still discover. I remember the day when *Sputnik* was launched by the Soviets. I was a student at Oxford, and a man of science— a professor at an observatory who had detected the waves generated by *Sputnik* in space—came to give a conference at our university. He told us that if we increased scientific knowledge, be it in the macrocosm or the microcosm, we could not help but be convinced that there is a force that surpasses us.

So I am optimistic, and I think that the development of science and progress can help us find a new, deeper relationship with God.

In your book In Search of Spiritual Life, *you say:*

> History is not something that is acquired, something
> static. History, human life, is a movement, a process of
> change, I would say, a process of growth. [...] We are the
> makers of history, not only spectators.

*The man who "makes history," the "builder of his destiny,"
these are definitions that go back to the secular humanism of the
Italian Renaissance of the end of the fourteenth century, born in
some ways as a counterbalance to a certain fatalism with respect
to the history that had characterized the Christian Middle Ages.
Is yours a* Christian *humanism?*

When I speak of man as an actor in history, or a "maker of
history," I am not thinking about a man separated from
God. Sometimes Christians, when starting from the idea
that God is all-powerful, that His providence guides
history and the fate of each man, have ended up in a sort
of fatalism, a passivity and a resignation that have nothing
to do with the true spirit of Christianity. The essence of
Christianity is love, which implies participation, engagement, action. If everything was decided and established in
advance, we would only be instruments. But, on the contrary, God has given us freedom, and we have the
responsibility to exercise that freedom, the responsibility
to *make* history. Dynamism, creativity and action are all
essential characteristics for the Christian.

We are often tempted to wait for institutions and situations to change. We want the world to change. But we
forget that for that to happen, we must change ourselves.
That change means moving from separation to unity, from

indifference to engagement, from apathy to action, from the particular to the universal. That is the spirit with which we must approach the twenty-first century.

To answer you question more directly, I would say that I believe in a humanism that is not opposed to the Christian faith, because we are certainly in God's hands, but at the same time, we have the full freedom and responsibility to act.

The end of the century

The expectations for the year 1000 in Europe were full of concerns but also full of authentic spiritual ferments. Today, on the eve of the new century and millennium, people are feeling a certain anxiety. There is a resurgence of ancient forms of millenarianism, new prophecies are appearing...

What do you think of the year 2000?

For me, there is no difference between the year 2000 and the year 1999! It is the same time, the same world, the same people. It's the same river that flows, the same sun that rises and sets, the same sky above us and the same earth under our feet. At the same time, these occasions make us more sensitive to our vocation. What is important here is the awareness that the Christian religion has lived two thousand years in a world often in turmoil, and despite all of the historical vicissitudes that the Church has endured, it has always been able to serve the people of God all over the world. So this millennium is an occasion for all Christians, without distinguishing their denominations, to find in that legacy of two thousand years a new source of inspiration and motivation.

I often say that these anniversaries are not only observed to give homage to the past. We must find a living force in that past because the past is not something that vanishes, but continues in our lives. One of the definitions of the Church that I like the most describes it as a "living memory." History is an operating force and not only an affair of museums or textbooks. That is why I think that two thousand years of Christian testimony is a great lesson for all the people and all the believers of today. Christianity is a book that is still being written.

How should believers await the year 2000? What are the challenges of the third millennium of Christianity?

I see two fundamental challenges for Christians in this jubilee. The first is responding to the will of our Lord, that we be united. We must not be One in the sense of being uniform; but we cannot help but be united in spirit and in service.

The second challenge is to renew the vivacity and the authenticity of our Christian faith. Sometimes, we do not think of our faith as being a part of our cultural patrimony, of our social habits, of the convictions that we have inherited. But to be Christian is not just a formal membership; it is an engagement. Jesus said to us, "Take up the cross and follow me." But often we follow Him without taking up the cross. We follow Him because it is good and natural to be Christian. What we need is an effort, a more generous gift from ourselves. Sacrifice is the supreme manifestation of love: Christ preached love, but He crowned it with the cross. And as Saint Gregory of Datev, an Armenian theologian from the fourteenth century, said: "The glory of God is first the cross of the Lord." Without that cross, we cannot talk about glory. I believe that the anniversary of the year 2000 must give us the strength of renewal, the strength to rediscover the authenticity of the first Christians, for whom the Word of God, before being the written word, was real life.

Progress and happiness

In the twentieth century, we saw both the exaltation of great ideals, of philosophical, social, economic and political systems — and their disappearance. Some figures who over the decades were seen as prophetic and incontestable have become quiet in the ideological scene of our era: philosophers, ideologists, revolutionaries, dictators...

The last few decades of the century and of the millennium have proven to be rather bizarre, especially in Europe. This century has been without doubt one of the bloodiest in our history (two World Wars, revolutions and military occupations, the despotism of the Left and the Right) and could be considered the century of division (between the East and West of the continent). Towards the end of the century, in the second half of the '80s, Europe experienced a moment of optimism and enthusiasm: the end of Communism, the fall of the Berlin Wall, the preparation of a political and economic union in the West. Unfortunately, the '90s disappointed many Europeans: new wars, the disintegration of certain countries, the slowdown of the economy. In several countries of the East, people were disappointed in the young democracies and turned, with nostalgia, towards the Communist past.

That very disappointment, after the enthusiasm of the '80s, affected interreligious ecumenism and dialogue. The lack of ideals and the disappointment engendered a pessimistic vision of our times, which accompanies the critique of industrial societies and the ideology of progress prevalent in post-modern thought.

What do you think of the disappointment of the end of the century?

I do not entirely share that presentation of the end of the century. I think that in our time, there are more positive aspects than people think. It is true that we are now experiencing a lack of great ideals, of eminent moral figures, and that is without a doubt a loss; but the disappearance of the ideologies and the social systems of the past can leave room for the rediscovery of true values.

For me, the most unfortunate aspect of modernity is that the advances in technology have swept aside intellectual, moral and spiritual values. What is dominant now is an uncontrolled technology, in which the inventor is beginning to become the victim of his invention. Technical progress without limits or a moral orientation runs the risk of undermining man's dignity.

I am not absolutely against scientific or technological progress. On the contrary, that progress might be the most evident proof of God's work in this world because, after all, who gave this power to man if not God? But we must develop our moral reflection on the value of technology and its use. The machine cannot *become* the master; the machine must *serve* its inventor, and man must always remain the master because it is the true happiness of humanity that is at stake.

In any case, it seems more and more clear to me that the world cannot follow that same path of blind determination towards a progress that is exclusively technological; in the so-called overdeveloped countries, people are living in an overabundance of material "well-being," and at the same time they are dissatisfied. People are wondering, "What is the meaning of life?" I have the firm conviction that this is the beginning of a spiritual renewal, which will characterize the third millennium.

Sometimes I ask myself if our superb technological development is truly such great progress. In the era of classical culture in Greece and Rome, when philosophy was born as the science of thought, those peoples who left us incomparable works of art did not have our technological progress. Were they less happy for it? Less human than we? I think that progress must be put in the context of the totality of human life. There are certainly great conquests made by human genius of which we are taking advantage, and we must encourage science and technology. But we must evaluate their contribution to the development of all men, and not only their rapidity, their efficiency.

Today, there is an imbalance between the development of technology, industry, and everything that has to do with consumption on the one side, and on the other side spiritual values, thought, and the arts. This imbalance must be corrected.

Overall, you think that spiritual and human development today is disproportionate to technological development. One could say that we are underdeveloped spiritually.

Yes. I think that we need to deepen our understanding of the human being. Who are we? We are very familiar with the exterior world, but we should not forget Socrates' lesson, the famous inscription on the Temple at Delphi: *Know thyself.* Dr. Alexis Carrel, who received the Nobel Prize in 1912, wrote a book entitled, *Man, the Unknown.* I think that that title has lost none of its pertinence. How can we live our lives in a way that will secure "shared happiness"? I believe that we must work towards the construction of a humanity that brings back the seal of the Creator.

The goal of progress is to help man secure happiness. Happiness, on the other hand, is exactly what all religions guarantee man.

I often say that progress consists in the comprehension of the Creator's design. We are not created for no reason; we are created for our full blossoming in joy. But to be happy does not imply egoism, withdrawal into oneself. On the contrary, to secure happiness means going outside of oneself, going toward others. In that sense, the responsibility towards the underprivileged, the needy, is for me a part of humanity's spiritual progress. Progress that is not imbued with spirituality, that does not share with those who are ridiculed in their human dignity, who are oppressed and exploited, is not true progress.

You are right to say that all religions share the goal of man's happiness. What is absolutely urgent and necessary today is that believers of all religions are tuned in to that common vocation and commit together to its actualization. Happiness can never be obtained in conflict, antagonism, hostility or hatred. On the contrary, the secret to happiness is in mutual love and respect. To vanquish the mortal threat of so many ethnic, political, economic and other confrontations and conflicts, all of the believers of the world must dedicate themselves, together, to peace.

One of the most striking paradoxes of our times is that in spite of the extraordinary development of communications, which should favor sharing between peoples, we are seeing a lack of unity between nations, which gives rise to the difference between poor and rich countries. Perhaps the spiritual progress that you envision works in terms of that development of unity?

Exactly. From unity to sharing. You know the story that the Lord told of the man who was attacked by thieves and left on the road. The priest and the Levite quickened their pace. The only person who showed his human solidarity was a Samaritan. That story is a concrete example of what sharing is: the solicitude toward others. That solicitude makes our happiness—and its absence makes our unhappiness. Happiness is always sharing. If we are imprisoned within ourselves, our family, our small world, then that happiness is not authentic.

From my personal perspective, for the unity of humanity to become a reality one day, it must be the focus of a relentless effort, rather than the dream or desire it currently is. The union of Europe is at our doorstep; the global vision of humanity as a single creation of God is becoming a common vision. To get there, I think that we must be motivated by a philosophy of true sharing. The North and the South, the East and the West, which have essentially become political, economical and sociological concepts, must reclaim, in our minds, their original geographic signification, as different parts of the same planet.

A bicyclist eyeing the finish line

Western society is becoming more and more a society of elderly people, as the average age is rising and the number of births is declining. The problems of senior citizenship, of the twilight of life, are faced today by millions of our contemporaries. What does old age signify in the life of men?

Old age is not a time of bitterness; it is a part of our human condition. At a certain time, a person's growth arrives at old age. The end of our existence on Earth is approaching, and it is true that that can cause fear: the elderly person can withdraw into pessimism, fatalism, his memories, the nostalgia of a past that will never return.... Personally, I think that an elderly person should feel like a bicyclist, who right at the moment of seeing the finish line, makes an effort, gives all that he can of himself.

Old age is a time when one sees things from the perspectives of remembrance and the preparation for death. That is why it is a very important time for every man. You can develop a mature way of thinking, see things more clearly, evaluate the meaning of life. Every real-life experience gives a person wisdom that must be used to serve others.

But old age also has a value in itself: it is the moment when you realize even more that life is God's gift, when you consider what you have done with that gift, what you haven't done, and what failures you have had. After evaluating your past, you can live the time that remains with a feeling of gratefulness toward God, even when you see that you have not carried out His will completely. You can thank God for the fact that even our faults have shaped us. The awareness of our failures can drive us to dedicate the time we have left to true values and to pass on this message to newer generations.

The aspect of passing on your knowledge in the course of your life is very important. It can happen that an elderly person hangs on to his life, to the times that have slipped through his fingers, to his diminishing faculties, and that he lives the last season of life with the regret of not having done certain things, of not having seen his plans through. I remember one of our catholicoi who, having reached the age of eighty and being close to death, had so many initiatives and ideas that if you had wished him ten more years of life, he would have said that it wouldn't be enough. He finished by saying to the students of the seminary: "I have not succeeded in realizing all of my plans; it is you who will continue them." We must arrive at the awareness that each of us offers a contribution, gives an impetus to a common work, which will be continued by others.

Tradition has it that the Apostle Saint John, already very advanced in age, would repeat to his disciples, "Love one another." And if they begged him to give them instructions, if they asked him to say something different, he would repeat, "Love one another." Holiness, you are a man of extraordinary vitality, and the rate at which you work is surprising. Over the years, you have exercised your ministry among the youth, and you often say that youth is not a question of age. In short, you may not have thought about leaving a "spiritual testament." Nevertheless, if someone asked you for the words that Karekin I would like to be remembered for in the future, what would you say?

Actually, I have never thought about a spiritual testament because, as you have already guessed, I still feel young. In any case, I would very much like to repeat what Saint John said. I would formulate those instructions in the following manner: "Be men, by keeping within yourself the presence of Him who created you. Do not betray our human nature, marked by the seal of the divine."

God is love; God created us in His image. Consequently, love is the most perfect realization for man. An artist cannot create if he does not love his creation. What is created without love cannot be valuable because hatred has never produced anything other than destruction. Love emanates from a person, which reflects the Creator. Love is our debt to God, which we can only repay by loving others.

The water of love finds its source in God, and as the water of a stream flows endlessly, we cannot keep love for ourselves, ignoring others: it is in the nature of love to not stop, to flow without end...

Behind the curtain

Very little time separates us from the end of the century and the millennium. If for a single moment we remove the curtain hiding the future from us, what do you see? The brilliant dawn of a happy humanity? The darkness of nothingness? The kingdom of heaven on Earth? Ecological devastation?

I see a dawn. I have great hope that the next century will be better than the present. I see indications of this, I would say, through a biblical expression, the *signs of the times*. Among the youth, there is a new awareness of their responsibility. There is, one might say, even a revolution *vis-à-vis* the injustices of our times. And if the youth is awakening, that is without doubt a positive sign for a better future. There are new spiritual movements, about which the media, unfortunately, speak very little.

If we stay within the sphere of a society dominated by materials, we renounce the depth of our humanity because that depth is the dimension in which we perceive the Creator's presence. It seems to me that we are beginning to understand that even if we are inventors, we are not *creators*, but *creatures*. If we have intelligence, it comes to us from Someone. That explains a certain religious renewal in recent times. I believe that it was André Malraux who said that the twenty-first century will be a religious century, or it will not be at all.

In short, you are optimistic?

Yes. Very optimistic.

ACKNOWLEDGEMENTS

Between Heaven and Earth was produced at the order of His Eminence Archbishop Khajag Barsamian, Primate of the Diocese of the Armenian Church of America, to honor the memory of His Holiness Karekin I, the 131st Catholicos of All Armenians. After the first edition appeared in France in 1998, His Holiness was eager to have the book translated into English. Archbishop Barsamian and the family and friends of His Holiness were anxious that this wish of our late Catholicos should become a reality.

St. Vartan Press would like to acknowledge those who contributed to this edition. Brian Wong provided a learned and sensitive English translation from the original French, and Iris Papazian edited the manuscript to prepare it for publication. Christopher Zakian designed the interior layout and supervised the editorial process. Elise Antreassian and Sona Panajyan contributed to various aspects of production. Armen Edgarian designed the cover and interior photo pages, featuring images by C. Der Boghosian (pp. *xviii*, 192), J. K. Hovhannes (pp. 72, 248), *L'Osservatore Romano* (p. 214). E. Masraff (p. 34), B. Zobian (pp. 128, 154, 178, 268). Michael Kane printed the volume.

A final debt of thanks must go to Professor Guaïta, not only for permitting St. Vartan Press to produce an English edition, but for conducting this remarkable interview in the first place. His Holiness' untimely death deprived his people of a wise and inspiring father, and deprived the world of what surely would have been a valuable personal memoir of his ministry. This interview will bring Catholicos Karekin's vast learning, no less than his unforgettable pastoral presence, to future generations.